NAVAL EIGHT

NAVAL EIGHT

A history of No. 8 Squadron
R.N.A.S.—afterwards No.208
Squadron R.A.F.—from its
formation in 1916 until the
Armistice in 1918.

LONDON :
Published by THE SIGNAL PRESS LTD., 133 Gt. Suffolk St., S.E.1.

1931

CONTENTS

LIST OF ILLUSTRATIONS

PREFACE

A year or two ago, the old members of No. 8 Squadron, R.N.A.S., decided to produce a history of their Squadron. When this decision came to be put into practical form, it was discovered that the best chance of producing a readable and interesting book lay in enlisting joint authors instead of entrusting the whole of the writing to one individual, the feeling being that no one man could adequately deal with every side of the Squadron's activities. Hence the form of the present volume.

It is hoped that, apart from its value to those who actually served with Eight Naval, the book will succeed in conveying to the non-service reader something of the atmosphere and duties of the Squadron. Every effort has been made to avoid technicalities and difficulties of a like description.

While this is called a "history," it does not pretend to be a complete history. Some names are mentioned, but the omission of any name is of no significance. Throughout the text, officers and men are described by the rank or rating which they held at the time.

It only remains for acknowledgments to be gratefully given to all those who by the offer or contribution of material or photographs made the compilation of the book possible. Thanks are also due to the Historical Section of the Air Ministry for invaluable assistance, and to the Printers, Messrs. The Signal Press, Limited, for their interest and co-operation.

E.G.J.

FOREWORD

By Air Vice-Marshal Sir Charles L. Lambe,
K.C.B., C.M.G., D.S.O.

FOREWORD

18th October, 1916.

"The Admiralty have decided, on the urgent representation of the Army Council, to detach at once a Squadron of eighteen Fighting Aeroplanes from the Dunkirk command for temporary duty with the British Expeditionary Force."

The above is an extract from an Admiralty letter to the Admiral commanding the Dover Patrol, and was responsible for the birth of No. 8 Naval Squadron (afterwards No. 208 Squadron).

The re-organisation of the Royal Naval Air Service at Dunkirk was commenced early in 1916, the original No. 1 Wing being expanded to Nos. 1, 4 and 5 Wings, and later these were re-organised into squadrons which specialised in the various kinds of work required such as Air Fighting, Spotting for the Navy and Reconnaissance, and Day and Night Bombing.

There was no squadron, however, with anything like the number of aeroplanes which formed the standard Royal Flying Corps Squadron, and consequently it was only possible to form No. 8 Naval by taking a Flight from each of the three Wings.

I believe, if my memory is correct, that every officer and man that formed the original Squadron was a volunteer and in a short time I had a very effective means of controlling excess of zeal and spirit by warning young officers generally that in the event of their being reported,

5

they would lose their chance of being sent down to work with No. 8.

Although I had had some previous conversations with Major General H. M. Trenchard, the General Officer commanding the R.F.C. in the Field, and was thoroughly aware of the urgent necessity for rendering assistance to the R.F.C., yet the above letter was the first official intimation I received, and, looking back, I think it is little less than a miracle that the Squadron actually was ready in time to go down to the Somme Battle Front on October 26th.

The life and history of this Squadron are set forth very fully in this book. So successful was this initial experiment of co-operation between the R.N.A.S and the R.F.C. that by December 1916, on the still more urgent appeals from the Army Council, the Admiralty had agreed to the raising of four additional Single Seater Squadrons at Dunkirk, to be lent to the Army. This co-operation between the two Services in the air was very thorough and no doubt was responsible for hastening the creation of the Royal Air Force. It may fairly be said that No. 8 played a most important part in the early stages of amalgamation of the two flying services.

I feel sure that this work will be of the greatest interest, not only to the original members of the Squadron and their relatives, but to the personnel of the Squadron at the present day and to those who come after.

CHARLES L. LAMBE,
Air Vice-Marshal.

CHAPTER I.

FORMATION AND EARLY
DAYS IN FRANCE

By Group Capt. G. R. Bromet, D.S.O., O.B.E., R.A.F.
(Squadron Commander R.N. with No. 8 Squadron, R.N.A.S.)

CHAPTER I

Formation and Early Days in France.

§ I.

During the second half of 1915, the re-organisation and expansion of the R.N.A.S. in the Dover Patrol was taking place in accordance with the plans of Wing Captain (now Air Vice-Marshal Sir) C. L. Lambe who had assumed Command of the Air Forces at Dover and Dunkirk in August, 1915. In order to carry out a vigorous offensive in the spring of 1916, he had obtained approval to increase the Air Forces in the Command to eight squadrons of 18 machines each, to have a central repair depot at Dunkirk, and to base a local defence and training squadron on Dover. Sites were chosen for aerodromes between Dunkirk and Bergues, and by April, 1916, No. 1 Wing was established at St. Pol, No. 5 at Coudekerque, and No. 4 Wing at Petite-Synthe. Whilst this expansion was taking place, Wing Captain Lambe had also succeeded in getting a new organisation approved which would bring the R.N.A.S. more into line with the R.F.C., and from this date onwards a flight became six machines, a squadron two or more flights, and a wing two or more squadrons.

During the summer of 1916, arrangements were made between Wing Captain Lambe and General Trenchard for R.N.A.S. squadrons to carry out a bombing programme in the northern area in order to divert air activity from the Somme front, and in the early autumn a further step was taken to relieve the pressure on the R.F.C. on this Front by obtaining Admiralty approval to lend a fighting squadron to the R.F.C., for duty on the Somme.

It was decided to form this squadron by taking one flight from each of the Dunkirk Wings, so No. 1 Wing provided six Sopwith "Pups," No. 4 Wing six "Nieuports," and No. 5 Wing six Sopwith "1½ Strutters."

It was my luck to be offered the Command of this Squadron, and from Guston Road Aerodrome at Dover on October 25th, 1916, I crossed to Dunkirk in H.M.S. *Nubian* (Commander N. R. Bernard) and reported for orders at Headquarters, R.N.A.S.

I was told that the Squadron was being attached to the 5th Brigade R.F.C., 22nd Wing, and that No. 32 Squadron, R.F.C., was being moved from the Aerodrome at Le Vert Galant, near Amiens, in order to make room for us.

On the following day I collected John D'Albiac (Lieut. R.M.A., and an Observer in No. 1 Wing) who had been appointed to the Squadron as Records Officer, and together we motored to Le Vert Galant by way of Bergues, Cassel, Hazebrouck, Forêt de Nieppe, St. Venant, Lillers, St. Pol, Frévent, Doullens and Beauval. We arrived about three in the afternoon and found Huskisson (my second in command) and Spurway (2nd Lieutenant, R.F.C., attached to us as Equipment Officer), with a small advance party of men, in possession and preparing for the arrival of the main party and the machines.

Our sheds (of which there were seven) and the Aerodrome lay on the right-hand side of the main Doullens-Amiens road, about 20 kilometres from Amiens. On the other side of this road, No. 23 Squadron, R.F.C. (F.E. 2B machines) had their Aerodrome. Our huts and billets were clustered round the four cross roads to the north of the sheds, and occupied the farmhouse and buildings belonging to one Monsieur Georges Bossu.

We were to be a Unit of the 5th Brigade, R.F.C. (Brigadier-General Longcroft), attached to the 5th Army (General Gough) operating in the region north of the river Ancre on a front of approximately ten miles.

The 5th Brigade, R.F.C., had their Headquarters at Toutencourt, and consisted of the 15th and 22nd Wings. The 22nd Wing, to which we were attached, had its Headquarters at Rosel Farm, within half a mile of our Aerodrome, and was commanded by Lieut.-Colonel T. C. R. Higgins, whose Adjutant was Captain Nicholson.

To return now to the happenings on the 26th. The weather, which had been cold and wet most of the day, cleared up at Dunkirk just before dusk and all the Flights took off. Unfortunately they started a bit too late and a number of machines got separated and landed in various parts of the country as darkness overtook them. The "Nieuport" Flight, ably led by Mackenzie, arrived only one short, and a "Pup," flown by Travers, also reached Vert Galant safely.

Meanwhile, our transport consisting of eight lorries, five tenders, a large trailer and a workshop lorry had arrived, but owing to darkness, mud, and pouring rain, it was decided to defer unloading until the morning, and we just tumbled out the bags and hammocks and got the men settled into their quarters for the night. Hammocks were slung in a large barn belonging to Monsieur Bossu's farm, and the men made themselves as comfortable as circumstances permitted—which is another way of saying that there was no comfort at all. There are better places than barns (and leaky ones at that) in which to sleep on a wet October night, but there are also worse places in war time, although you wouldn't have got any of our "braves" to believe that at reveillé on October 27th.

Further along the road, in the Officers' billet, things were not too comfortable either. The departure of the machines from Dunkirk in the afternoon had not been anticipated and when the pilots started to come in, some with and others without their machines, we had neither kit, quarters, nor food ready for them. Eventually some fourteen hungry, cold, and tired Subs had collected in Monsieur Bossu's parlour all demanding everything we hadn't got, and the entertainment was complete. In the end we got them sorted out and sent to No. 23 Squadron for meals, after which we unearthed their traps and sent them to find their sleeping quarters as best they could.

The morning of the 27th broke with rain driving against our windows and with a steady drip through the roof of the barn. If the men felt as miserable as they looked, they must have been miserable indeed, and their cheerfulness was not increased by finding only tea and dry bread for breakfast. However, we soon got them too busy to worry over such matters and the day was spent in detailing quarters, arranging about rations, unloading stores, and sending out parties to the stranded machines. The Squadron was visited by Major-General Trenchard, accompanied by Colonel Hudson (No. 2, A.D.), Major Spicer (No. 5, A.A.P), Captain Corballis, and Lieutenant Maurice Baring. The General, with his accustomed concern for the well-being of Officers and men, made us feel at home right away, and with the thoroughness for which he had become famous, set about satisfying himself that we were *au fait* with the supply and repair facilities in the Field, and that we had everything we wanted. The General's "Make a note of it, Baring," with which we were to become so familiar, was heard for the first time.

By the 29th we had accounted for all machines, but two "Pups" and a 1½ Strutter were still out in the country.

The H.Q. Flight Officers' Mess was still in a rough and tumble condition. We boasted but one knife, fork, plate and cup for eight people and we had a standing diet of bully beef and biscuits. Nevertheless we were all superbly happy, and after the comfort of the Dunkirk Aerodrome mud and bully beef had a spice of adventure about them. During the next few days we had visits from General Gough, Brig.-General Longcroft, Wing Captain Lambe, Squadron Commander C. L. Courtney (O.C. No. 4 Wing, R.N.A.S.), and Major Moore-Brabazon. The latter brought a Gun Camera for practice with Lewis guns.

The 3rd November marked the first job of work over the lines, four Nieuports doing a line patrol Bouzincourt — Chateau-de-la-Haie, but without coming across any Huns. The idea of these patrols was to protect artillery machines, and at this time it was usual to do them with machines working in pairs and at a height varying from 1,000 to 8,000 feet.

On the afternoon of the 6th November I was messing about in the farm yard, going round the workshops, etc., when a small cavalcade consisting of a General, and two Staff Officers, and headed by four troopers with lances, drew rein in front of the barn, and I recognised General Sir Douglas Haig. The Commander-in-Chief dismounted and asked to be shown the machines. He took the keenest interest in everything and was particularly anxious to meet Officers and have a word with them.

The weather continued very bad, and on the 7th I motored to Acheux (in search of the Field Cashier and money), then to Senlis (in search of timber), and on to Puchevillers (in search of lunch and information about Aircraft Parks).

The 5th Army Aircraft Park was situated at Puchevillers, under the Command of Major Spicer, R.F.C.

At this time each Army had its A.A.P., which was a mobile organisation keeping a stock of aircraft and engine spares just sufficient to maintain all squadrons in the Brigade, and doing all plane repairs. For plane repairs, No. 5, A.A.P. had converted an orchard into a workshop, and the Section was so highly organised that it could repair one complete set of planes per day.

November 9th and 10th were interesting days for the Squadron. On November 9th, 48 hours' flying was done, and on the 10th, 36 hours. Eleven combats took place and the Squadron got its first Hun. This was a "Roland" shot down over Bapaume by Flight Sub.-Lieut. Galbraith, flying Sopwith "Pup" No. 5193.

The following extracts from the Squadron Diary give very good illustrations of the trials, difficulties and triumphs which went to make up a day's flying at this period of the war :—

"Very fine morning. Mackenzie and Corbett did the first line patrol from 6.15 to 8.30. Mackenzie got close behind a German machine like a 'L.V.G.' and opened fire, but his gun jambed after firing only a few shots. Hope, Goble, Compston, Wood and Lawson, all had scraps with other machines but four out of five had jambs in their guns, so had to break off the fight. Patrols and formation flying were carried out in the afternoon. Thom, on landing in his '1½ Strutter' hit a farm implement in one corner of the aerodrome and wrecked his machine. Galbraith has just come in from No. 7 Squadron where he had made a forced landing owing to engine failure. He had two scraps with Hun machines and in both cases he saw the observers killed.

"Nice fine morning. Line patrol by '1½ Strutters' at 6 a.m. Nieuport scouts tested guns before breakfast. Grange had two fights with German machines and he thinks he killed the observer of one of them. Grange's machine had both the front inter-plane struts shot through. Trapp went with Grange on this patrol and was missing until about 3.30. It appeared that he saw a machine about to dive on Grange when the latter was attacking another, and so he turned to attack this one and had a chase of about 30 minutes before getting close enough to attack. Eventually, the Hun machine broke off the engagement and Trapp steered N.W. until he fetched up at Dieppe. Here he got a re-fill of oil and petrol, and arrived back at Vert Galant at 3.30. Galbraith went up on the same patrol in the afternoon met five "Roland" bi-planes south of Arras. These he attacked and brought one down. Three of our machines were ordered over to Marieux to escort a Wireless B.E. 2C. Unfortunately, Booker's machine (a '1½ Strutter') crashed on landing, owing to the wind-indication on the ground being wrongly placed. The other machines did not go on the escort duty after all owing to engine failure of the B.E. 2C. Five Nieuports went on an offensive patrol with some De Havilands in the afternoon but nothing of interest occurred.

"Fine bright day and a lot of flying done. Goble shot down a German machine in the morning in the region of Gomiecourt. In the afternoon six 'Pups' arrived from Dunkirk to replace the 1½ Strutters. In the afternoon many patrols were carried out, and Galbraith brought down a German machine near Miraumont. Very cold weather and several pilots suffering from frost bite on the face."

The month of November was made up of days similar to the above, interspersed with periods of very bad weather, sometimes fog but more often wind and rain.

Our first casualty occurred on November 23rd when Hope failed to return from an offensive patrol. We heard subsequently that he died of wounds, in Germany.

On December 1st, we lost the services of Galbraith who had a breakdown in health and was sent away for a rest. He came to the Squadron with an established reputation as a fighting pilot and his work with us was beyond praise. No Hun retreated too far behind the line and no formation was too formidable for this stout hearted Canadian to attack. He had remarkable courage and brains and, although a curious sort of fellow who took a bit of understanding, he was a jolly good chap right through.

November ended and December began with a succession of fogs, but we had a fine spell on the 4th, and a busy day. We started off by providing an escort for a bomb raid by No. 23 Squadron. The objective was an aerodrome near Bahagnies and the bombing force consisted of eight F.E.s each carrying four 20-lb. Hales bombs with an escort of three Sopwith "Pups" flying at 13,000 feet, and four De Haviland "Pusher" Scouts from No. 32 Squadron flying at 10,000 feet. After the raid, the bombing formation, accompanied by Goble and Little in Sopwith "Pups," did an offensive patrol over the area Mory, Morchies, Velu and Ytres. Never previously had there been so many Huns about and Goble and Little were scrapping all the forenoon. Goble got one down and forced others to land and also broke up several formations. The cold was intense, and to add to Goble's discomfort, he was continually sick. So this morning's work was particularly praiseworthy. We heard nothing of Little until long after he was due back, and then he just blew in from nowhere, as was his wont. Apparently whilst fighting a "Halberstadt" his gun had jambed and he was forced to land close to our trenches. He managed to clear the jamb, went up again, had another scrap or two, and then, having brought a Bosche down, decided that honour was satisfied, and that he had better find his way home again.

On the afternoon patrol we lost Corbett. We heard afterwards that in a fight with two enemy machines, near Belville Wood, he brought one down and was then himself killed in the air. A fine youngster he was—only 18—with the heart of a lion, and all the attributes which

18

go to make a successful fighting pilot. He had become a general favourite in the Squadron and his loss was keenly felt. He was buried on December 6th in the C.C.S. Cemetery at Heilly.

The rehearsals were now in full swing for our Christmas Revue, Mr. Brice and Leading Mechanic Black being the foremost figures in the enterprise. On non-flying days we were managing to keep ourselves fit with rugger and soccer matches, and we were doing pretty well.

The fogs during the first few days of December were followed by bad weather throughout almost the entire month, and it was a very trying time for all the pilots. On December 10th we had a very bad crash on the aerodrome, resulting in the death of Trapp. He had his "Sopwith" up for a test flight and, on pulling out of a very steep dive, the machine folded up. He was a splendid type of Canadian whom everybody liked, and he was an exceptionally courageous and brilliant fighting pilot. He was buried at Beauval on December 11th.

The weather continued bad right up to Christmas and for once in a way one was relieved to find a dud morning when Christmas day broke. As the conditions removed all doubt as to whether to send machines off on jobs or not, one was able to lie back and enjoy one's day. I remember going to Church in the morning, having an enormous meal in the middle of the day, preceded by rounds of the mess decks, playing soccer in the afternoon, and taking part in a Smoking Concert in the transport hangar at night. December ended true to its reputation, and I find in my Diary nothing but references to low clouds and very strong winds. On the night of the 31st, most of us went up to No. 23 Squadron's Mess and saw the New Year in.

In the New Year Promotions List, Mackenzie went up to Flight Commander, and Thom, Booker, Compston, Wood, Todd, and Grange to Flight Lieutenants. O'Hagan was promoted to Lieutenant R.N.V.R. We played No. 5 Squadron at Rugger on the 3rd and beat them 11 points to nil, and then in the evening we held our Concert in the transport hangar. General Longcroft and about 400 Officers and men saw the show, and we had a topping evening ending up with a cheery supper party in "A & B" Flight Mess. Those who were there will remember the punch brewed by Franks and how the Brigade Major—that best of fellows, Captain Walker—brought about his downfall by mixing beer with it.

Here is the recipe :—

"THE GENERAL'S" HOT RUM PUNCH. MARK 1.

> 6 Lemons.
> 1 Pint Rum.
> ½ Bottle Brandy.
> ½ Bottle Curaçao.

Add a Port glass full of Mixed Liqueurs.
Squeeze lemons and sugar in one bowl, Rum and Brandy in second bowl, and Curaçao and all Liqueurs in third bowl.

When all are well mixed up put contents of first and second bowls into number three, add boiling water according to taste, and bring the Punch to a *simmer, not to boiling point.*

Add a topping of grated Nutmeg or slices of Lemon.

I don't think anybody enjoyed January very much. The cold was intense and from the 8th to the 22nd we had bad weather with a lot of snow, and only on two occasions was any flying possible, and then only test and practice flights. This period of idleness was very trying for all concerned. The pilots needed a rest, it is true, but they had been rather shaken recently by a series of casualties, and the last thing they really wanted was cold and depressing weather with nothing to do but to sit over the fire, talk war, and get mouldy. It is to their everlasting credit that they got through this bad patch without loss of keenness or morale, and it was more apparent than ever to me that I had the support of the finest crowd of fellows ever. Flying was resumed on January 23rd in intensely cold weather with snow lying thick on the ground, and work went on over the lines every day until the end of the month. A biting east wind with from 15 to 20 degrees of frost during the day, and much colder at night, made everybody sit up, and on top of this the days were not being lucky ones for the Squadron. There were not a lot of Huns about, but the ones that did come over were showing more boldness and they were making a practice of crossing our lines to take photographs, and to do artillery work. Try as we might, we hadn't been able to bring any down, and we had annoyed Generals and other people, and had ourselves been very much annoyed, thereby. On the 24th of January Mackenzie failed to return from an offensive patrol and we learnt eventually from the German Air Service that he had been brought down in combat and buried at Achiet-le-Grand, near Bapaume. I find it quite impossible to express adequately my admiration for this splendid Officer and great gentleman. In the air, a fine pilot and a brainy and courageous leader who inspired immediate and lasting confidence, and whom the Flight would follow anywhere. On the ground, a keen student of air tactics and fighting methods, a first-class organiser, a loyal and able Officer and the life and soul of any Mess. Small wonder that he was a universal favourite and that we looked upon his loss as irreparable.

Luck seemed to have temporarily deserted us, and we felt it keenly because the Squadron was due for relief early in February, and we wanted particularly to finish up with a roar. Instead of that, we had a very anxious time, and although several combats took place, no more Huns were accounted for.

Mackenzie's loss on the 24th was followed by Woods having to go away owing to a breakdown in health, and we had Soar adrift for twelve hours on the 26th, and Shaw missing for the same period on the following day. Fortunately both of them turned up, but at the time we thought they had gone. To add to these misfortunes, the weather remained intensely cold and several of the pilots were suffering from severe colds and from frost-bite. We continued

Squadron-Commander
G. R. BROMET,
D.S.O., R.N.

Squadron-Commander
C. DRAPER,
D.S.C., R.N.

Flight-Commander
B. L. HUSKISSON,
D.S.C., R.N.

Flight-Commander
S. Q. GOBLE,
D.S.O., D.S.C., R.N.

our work over the lines until February 2nd, when we were relieved by Mulock's Squadron (No. 3). The new Squadron took over all our machines and we returned to Dunkirk by road on the 3rd.

And so ended the first phase, and I think this is the moment to sound the "Still" in order to give a thought and a cheer to our very splendid Ship's Company. One knows that all the time it was hats off to C.P.O.s Rosling and Scott, and to one and all on the "Lower Deck" whose single thought from the word go had been to do their damnedest for the good name and the efficiency of the Squadron. There had been times when life had little to offer beyond discomforts and difficulties : wet billets, frozen guns, fractious engines, trials of the road, and all the rest of it. But with all hands pulling together as our fellows pulled, these times passed practically unnoticed—they certainly left no mark. Said Sir Douglas Haig: "The care of the machines has been above reproach and the discipline of the Unit very good," and with these words as a record of how well they had done their job the men of the Squadron moved off along the road to Dunkirk.

§ II.

The Squadron remained at Dunkirk, giving leave and being re-equipped until the 15th February, when it moved to Furnes and took over the aerodrome from Naval Squadron No. 1 on their transfer to the Somme. During the rest period at Dunkirk "C" Flight had been taken away to form the nucleus of a new Squadron (Naval Squadron No. 9), and a number of changes had also occurred amongst pilots.

On March 13th, Huskisson left to take Command of Naval Squadron No. 4, and he took with him as Stores Officer B. C. Bennett, until recently an A.C. II in the Squadron, and now W.O. II. He got promoted straight up to Warrant Officer and, although he had to stand a lot of chaff about his somewhat freakish promotion, nobody earned it better. Arnold (A. R.) relieved Huskisson, and other changes were Cook to No. 4 Wing, Branford and Shaw to No. 9 Squadron, and Thom and Hervey to Nos. 10 and 9 Squadrons respectively as Acting Flight Commanders.

Our job at Furnes consisted of fighter patrols to attack enemy aircraft threatening the Dunkirk area, strafing kite balloons, watching train movements in the Ostend district, escorting French photographic machines, protecting their artillery machines, and generally making ourselves useful to our friends and offensive to the enemy. During this period also, we were taking delivery of "Sopwith" triplanes (130 h.p. "Clerget" engines).

The French with whom we came in contact at Furnes were the 29th Division (General Rouquerol) at Coxyde, and Escadrilles F.36 (Capitaine F. Walckenaer) and C.226 (Capitaine des Isnards). And one remembers a very charming Intelligence Officer, Lieut. Boulanger, with whom we had many dealings.

We remained at Furnes until March 27th, when we were relieved by Breese's Squadron (No. 10), and left to join the 1st Brigade and 10th Wing, R.F.C., on the 1st Army Front.

On the day before we left Furnes, Prince Alexander of Teck and Major O'Connor, who was on his Staff at the Headquarters of the British Mission at La Panne, came and had tea with us, and after dinner that night the Huns had the bombing fever and kept us in and out of dug-outs until past midnight. Very inconsiderate of them because we had to be up at 5 a.m. the next day for some special operations against Zeebrugge before proceeding to our new aerodrome.

We didn't make a lucky start from Furnes. First of all the weather caused delays, then Compston and Pailthorpe damaged their machines on landing at Auchel because the wind indicator had been wrongly laid out, then on the following day Preston crashed badly when taking off from Furnes and had to go into La Panne Hospital; and finally Hammond lost his way, made a forced landing near the lines, and crashed his machine.

Still, we quickly forgot these little worries and we were very soon settled comfortably into our new quarters and eager to let the Huns try conclusions with the triplanes. Our new aerodrome was just off the main road between Lozinghem and Auchel, west of Bethune and about twelve miles from the lines, and adjoined No. 25 Squadron R.F.C. aerodrome.

We were now attached to the 1st Army (General Horne), and a Unit of 1st Brigade, R.F.C. (Brigadier-General Shepherd), and 10th Wing, R.F.C. (Lieut.-Col. W. R. Freeman). The weather remained very bad — gales and snow-storms — until April 5th, so we occupied ourselves exchanging visits with neighbouring Squadrons, cultivating a few vegetables, and doing some practice flights. Some of our pilots hadn't got the hang of the triplanes yet, and minor crashes were a daily occurrence.

"Rattey" Chambers, who had just become liaison Officer at R.F.C. Headquarters, came over one day, and we had a visit from the Army Commander and his Chief-of-Staff (Major-General Anderson).

It wasn't until April 5th that the weather cleared up sufficiently to allow serious work over the lines to be started, and then the efforts of all Squadrons on this Front were concentrated on preparing the way for the Vimy Ridge push, the attack on which was launched at 5.30 a.m. on April 9th. Our neighbours, No. 25 Squadron, R.F.C., created a record on Easter Sunday, April 8th, by doing eighty hours flying with fourteen pilots, and by taking 237 photographs over the lines.

Our pilots soon got into their stride, and Little in particular had been making full use of his time since operations started on this Front. Two combats of his deserve special mention as showing his dash and ingenuity. The first concerns a Bosche artillery machine and a gun jamb.

One day, whilst on his own near Arras, he saw a two-seater enemy machine doing artillery work. After firing a few rounds at it he had a gun jamb. He tried to clear it and failed, but, instead of going away and leaving the fellow to carry on his work undisturbed, he decided to act as though his gun was O.K., and by constantly diving on the Hun kept the observer busy firing at him instead of being able to get along with his proper job. His dives and zooms away were so persistent and annoying that the Hun soon tired of the game and cleared off. Having watched him safely away, Little landed at a convenient spot near Arras, cleared his gun jamb, and went up again to look for further trouble.

The second combat concerned a crowd of "Albatross" Scouts, and the incident, as related by eye-witnesses in the Anti-Aircraft Artillery Group of the 3rd Army, is as follows :

"At 6.45 p.m. on 7/4/1917, a Sopwith Triplane, working alone, attacked eleven hostile machines, almost all 'Albatross' Scouts, N.E. of Arras. He completely out-classed the whole patrol of hostile machines, diving through them and climbing above them. One 'Albatross' Scout, painted red, which had been particularly noticed by this Section, dived on to him and passed him. The Sopwith dived on him and then easily climbed again above the whole patrol, drawing them all the time towards the Anti-Aircraft guns. As soon as they were in range, the Anti-Aircraft guns opened fire on the patrol, which turned eastward, and the Sopwith returned safely. The Officers who witnessed the combat report that the manœuvring of the Sopwith triplane completely out-classed that of the 'Albatross' Scout."

The days immediately following the launching of the attack on the Arras-Lens front were pretty bad for flying, and I remember one day in particular when some of the machines were caught in a snowstorm and had a bad time of it getting back over the lines. We had had some snow- and hail-storms during the forenoon, but in the middle of the afternoon the wind changed and the weather became fine with no indication of further storms. No. 25 Squadron had some urgent photographs to get, and as the job would take them some distance over the lines, we were asked to provide an escort. Arnold, Little, Booker, Cuzner, and Crundall went with them, but no sooner had they left than the weather broke again, and we had a succession of heavy snowstorms. We had an anxious time waiting for the machines to return. Eventually, Little and Arnold found the aerodrome, but we heard nothing of the others until after dark when all reported as having landed safely at various aerodromes round about. As it was snowing up to 8,000 feet, and the wind was of gale force at times, they did well to get down without damage.

The push had been going well, and on the 1st and 3rd Army Fronts about 11,000 prisoners had been taken up to April the 11th.

A "Special Order of the Day" issued by the C.-in-C. reads as follows :

"GENERAL HEADQUARTERS,

12th April, 1917.
"The Field-Marshal Commanding-in-Chief desires to express to all ranks his great satisfaction on the important successes achieved on the 9th instant by the First and Third Armies. The manner in which the

operations were prepared and carried out reflects the greatest credit on Commanders, Staffs and troops.

"The capture of the renowned Vimy Ridge is an achievement of the highest order of which Canada may well be proud.

"The performance of the VI, VII, and XVII Corps of the Third Army in surmounting the difficulties which confronted them is proof of very great skill and gallantry.

"The Royal Artillery, Heavy, Siege, and Field, by its untiring efforts and accurate fire prepared the way for and supported the advance of the infantry in the most efficient manner.

"The splendid work of the Royal Flying Corps under very adverse weather conditions, and in face of most determined opposition, has contributed largely to the success of the operations and calls for the highest praise.

"The Heavy Branch of the Machine Gun Corps has been of material assistance and has, under difficult circumstances, played a useful part.

"The Cavalry Corps and Corps Mounted Troops have taken the fullest advantage of such openings for cavalry action as the course of the operations has so far afforded.

"The Royal Engineers, both in the field and in their work behind the line, have carried out their many duties with the thoroughness and efficiency in which they are never found wanting; while all the various special Corps and Services which took part in the battle, as well as the Administrative Services and Departments on which the Armies depend for their maintenance, have taken their full share in bringing within reach the great successes gained.

"The Second, Fourth, and Fifth Armies have played their part admirably in keeping the enemy employed on their respective fronts, while to the Fourth and Fifth Armies in particular belongs the credit of having opened the way for these fresh successes by their splendid achievements on the Somme and the Ancre.

"The Commander-in-Chief desires to convey his warmest congratulations to all ranks of the Armies which he has the honour to command on the great successes already achieved by their untiring and self-sacrificing efforts, and on the prospects of further successes which have been opened."

All the time our pilots were being kept hard at it doing offensive patrols, and escorts for No. 25 Squadron. We got on extraordinarily well with this Squadron, and, although escort work was always difficult and unpopular with the fighter pilots, our fellows had the greatest admiration for the photographic work being carried out on the "F.E.s," and it was realised that one of our most important jobs was to see that these machines did their work unmolested.

On the 14th of April, Booker's Flight put up a particularly good show, and so well did they scrap that six machines of No. 25 Squadron took a set of photographs of the Mericourt-Oppy line, without being attacked at all. On the same day No. 25 Squadron had an astonishing story to tell about a combat in which one of their machines was engaged. The machine was attacked by three Huns and almost at once the observer was killed; a bullet then hit the petrol tank and the machine burst into flames. The pilot managed to get his burning machine down into a wood and with his clothes on fire was shot out clear and into a bush. The bush was set on fire by his clothes but he succeeded in rolling clear and putting his clothes out. He then made his way to the nearest British post, got in touch with the gunners and gave them the exact position of a battery which was active and doing a lot of damage. As the result of his information the hostile battery was silenced. It would be difficult to find a story of bravery and devotion to duty to beat this.

By April the 20th, the offensive had died down, but our advance had gone so well that Brigade H.Q. were in a position to consider moving their squadrons forward. In company with the O.C. 10th Wing, I hunted for possible sites for a new aerodrome for us, including Chateau-de-la-Haie, and the land along the Gouy-Servins-Carency road, but we could not find anything suitable in this area. At the beginning of May, a good site was found at Mont St. Eloi and after using this as an advanced landing ground for a short time, it was decided to erect a camp there and to move the whole Squadron as soon as possible.

On April 24th, we had the misfortune to lose Walter who was killed near Bailleul in a scrap with three "Albatross" Scouts. On the same day we had a splendid view of a fight in which the principals were Little, in a "Sopwith" triplane, a "Nieuport" from No. 40 Squadron, and a two-seater "Aviatick." The Hun was sighted over the aerodrome at about 10,000 feet and Little went up after him. A "Nieuport" appeared about the same time and both British machines got into action with the enemy at 12,000 feet, between our aerodrome and Bailleul. After scrapping for about twenty minutes, during which time the enemy machine was being forced lower and lower, Little managed to get a shot into the "Aviatick's" petrol tank, and the last we saw of the fight was the Hun diving down over the Bois de Revillion followed at a terrific pace by the "Sopwith" and the "Nieuport." This fight had an amusing finish. Forced down owing to loss of petrol the enemy machine landed without damage in a field at Les Facons. A few seconds later Little followed, and, in his haste, made a rough landing and turned upside down. The "Nieuport" did exactly the same thing, and when Little crawled out of his machine to claim his prisoner, the German pilot saluted smartly and said in English: "It looks as if I have brought you down, not you me, doesn't it." The machine was a brand new one with a 200 "Benz" engine and had come over to take photographs of St. Eloi aerodrome, and the area around Bethune. The pilot's name was Neumuller and the observer's, Huppertz. During the fight, the latter had got himself hopelessly entangled in his machine gun belt, and after the machine had landed, it took Little and Neumuller quite a time to free him. Neumuller said he thought the war ought to be over during the summer because England was starving. He was very surprised when at lunch at No. 1 Balloon Wing Headquarters a large plate of meat was put in front of him.

On the 26th, I motored with O'Hagan to find the place where Walter crashed, and on the following day he was buried close to an 18-pounder battery near the Bois-de-la-Maison Blanche, Sheet 51.B b.27, and we marked his grave with a cross made out of a propeller. C. P. O. Scott and a party of machines got a good dusting while salving the machine, but they got both airframe and engine back all right.

On the 29th we had the misfortune to lose Cuzner. The Canadians reported having seen a triplane brought down near Courrieres and, as the air was stiff with Huns that evening, it seemed probable that he had got separated from his formation and been attacked by superior numbers.

On the following morning we had a stroke of luck and an early wild goose chase after some supposed bombers led to a real field day. We were awakened early by the sound of bombs being dropped somewhere quite close and, in quick time, four machines were got away in chase. The bombers weren't seen but this was hardly surprising because it was misty; besides, there was the possibility that they were British machines dropping their eggs in the wrong place! However, away went our fellows over the lines and fell in with a whole party of Huns. Little and Compston each got two and Booker one.

On May 1st, Roach was killed in combat and Shields was brought down in our lines and severely injured. I saw Shields in the Casualty

Clearing Station at Barlin next day and he told his story. Having got separated from his formation he was returning home when he sighted and attacked a Hun near our lines. During the scrap he was taken unawares by a whole Flight of Albatross Scouts and he had to stunt for his life. With his machine badly hit about and driven low over Vimy Ridge he finally lost control and crashed in a spin. Luckily he was thrown clear, and, although he had a broken leg and other injuries, he managed to crawl into a shell-hole near by. Shelling was continuous during the day and he was forced to remain in the shell-hole in the heat of the sun, and in great pain from his injuries, from half past nine until four p.m., when he was found by three Tommies and removed to the C.C.S.

Round about this date, we had visits from Staff Paymaster Ricci, better known as "Bartimeus," who had come from Dunkirk to get copy for some stories about the R.N.A.S., and from Major Orpen, the well-known portrait painter.

Our move to the new aerodrome at St. Eloi was made on May 16th. A good aerodrome we thought it, and about the right distance from the "War"—14,500 yards from Oppy and 11,000 yards from Lievin. Here all ranks were under canvas, and the machines in Bessoneau hangars.

Our duties had been altered somewhat and the main task given us now was to strafe enemy artillery machines and any H.A. working on or near the lines. We found artillery machines most elusive and high flying two-seaters extraordinarily difficult to get to, but it was interesting work, and there was no lack of opportunities for ordinary Hun getting because the Squadron invariably did one offensive patrol a day, and often more.

On the 23rd May, "A" Flight, ably led by Simpson, had a big scrap with eleven Albatross Scouts within sight of the aerodrome. "C" Flight went up to help them but couldn't get there in time to be of much use, and although our fellows stuck to it splendidly, they were outnumbered and got badly knocked about. We lost Pailthorpe, and had Hall wounded. Bennett's machine was shot about badly and he himself had a marvellous escape. The day ended with a sporting attempt by a Hun to bomb our aerodrome. Booker's Flight had just landed when the shout went up "Hun at 3,000 feet approaching the aerodrome." At the same moment all the A.A. for miles round (including our Lewis guns) opened up on him, and Booker, Soar, and McCudden jumped into their machines and were away after him. The Hun turned for home as soon as he saw he had been spotted but our fellows caught him over Souchez and gave him a hot time. In the failing light he made good his escape and was last seen over Lens—a thrilling episode which did credit to both sides.

On the following day Smith failed to return from an offensive patrol.

On May 28th Mr. Brice, who had been our Stores Officer since the Squadron formed, left on posting to Dover. He was succeeded by Mr.

Fellows, an old acquaintance of mine at the Bristol Flying School at Larkhill where he was the Chief Instructor's Clerk when I learned to fly in 1913.

Other moves about this time were Simpson to a Flight-Commander's job in Naval Squadron No. 9, and Thompson (J. H.) and Jordan to the Squadron from No. 11 (Naval).

The battle of Messines had started on June 7th and although it was primarily a Second Army affair we were close enough to the fighting to make things strenuous and interesting. Also we had lent Johnston and Macdonald to No. 1 (Naval) to help them through the hard flying days during the push.

The C.-in-C.'s inspiring and encouraging "Special Order of the Day," dated 8th June, read as follows :—

"The complete success of the attack made yesterday by the Second Army, under the Command of General Sir Herbert Plumer, is an earnest of the eventual final victory of the Allied cause.

"The position assaulted was one of very great natural strength, on the defences of which the enemy had laboured incessantly for nearly three years. Its possession overlooking the whole of the Ypres Salient was of the greatest tactical and strategical value to the enemy.

"The excellent observation which he had from this position added enormously to the difficulty of our preparations for the attack, and ensured to him ample warning of our intentions. He was therefore fully prepared for our assault and had brought up reinforcements of men and guns to meet it.

"He had the further advantage of the experience gained by him from many previous defeats in battles such as the Somme, the Ancre, Arras, and Vimy Ridge. Out of the lessons to be drawn from these he had issued carefully thought-out instructions.

"Despite all these advantages, the enemy has been completely defeated. Within the space of a few hours all our objectives were gained, with undoubtedly very severe loss to the Germans. Our own casualties were, for a battle of such magnitude, most gratifyingly light.

"The full effect of this victory cannot be estimated yet, but that it will be very great, is certain.

"Following on the great successes already gained, it affords final and conclusive proof that neither strength of position nor knowledge of and timely preparation to meet impending assault can save the enemy from complete defeat, and that brave and tenacious as the German troops are, it is only a question of how much longer they can endure the repetition of such blows.

"Yesterday's victory was due to causes which always have given and always will give success, viz., the utmost skill, valour and determination in the execution of the attack following on the greatest forethought and thoroughness in preparation for it.

"I desire to place on record here my deep appreciation of the splendid work done, above and below ground as well as in the air, by all Arms, Services, and Departments, and by Commanders and Staffs by whom, under Sir Herbert Plumer's orders, all means at our disposal were combined, both in preparation and execution, with a skill, devotion and bravery beyond all praise.

"The great success gained has brought us a long step nearer to the final, victorious end of the War, and the Empire will be justly proud of the troops which have added such fresh lustre to its arms."

During the next week or two we were kept very busy making life a burden to enemy artillery machines and high flying two-seaters.

"The Summary of Work" for the period 3rd to 16th June said:

"The greater part of our work this fortnight has been in connection with Enemy Artillery Machines, and high flying two-seater machines (mostly Aviatick type) attempting reconnaissance of the back areas. Few Offensive Patrols, in comparison with our earlier work, have been carried out, and very few enemy scouts have been seen. It invariably happens that when conditions are most favourable for Artillery Registration, they are equally good for high reconnaissance, and owing to the number of fast and good climbing two-seaters which have regularly crossed our lines, we have not been able to give all our attention to Artillery machines, and consequently their work has not been interfered with quite so much as we had hoped for. However, over fifty Special Missions in search of spotting machines have been carried out, and Special W/T report that enemy machines ceased their calls abruptly on forty occasions.

"Two-seater L.V.G. and Aviatick reconnaissance machines have been very difficult to attack with success, owing to their very fine performance and the fact that they do their work singly and very high. At first we tried to stop them by sending up a machine whenever one was sighted or reported to be crossing our lines, but this policy proved a failure owing to the height and frequency with which they came over. The scheme of keeping one or two machines continually on Line Patrol from 8 a.m. to noon, between Lens and Arras at 15,000 feet or over, was then adopted and proved very successful. The number of enemy machines to cross our lines was considerably reduced, and those which did cross rarely got back without a fight.

"The Aviatick has proved a most difficult machine to bring down, and although many have been heavily and closely engaged and must have been badly hit, only five are known to have been brought down—two of which were on our side of the lines. On two occasions fights have taken place at 19,000 feet and over, and it is the rule rather than the exception for engagements with these two-seaters to start at 17,000 feet or over."

The 12th of June was a good day. Compston shot down an Albatross Scout close on the other side of the lines; then a Booker-Jenner Parson-Soar combination strafed an Aviatick over Arras (the remains of which Whitehead collected and took to No. 1 A.D.); and finally Soar got one down single handed S.E. of Arras.

On June 19th we had a surprise visit from Admiral Lord Charles Beresford. I remember his pride and interest at seeing the White Ensign flying and his farewell remark to me: "Give my respects to all your officers and tell them to keep up the old traditions."

On the following day the First Army Troops held their Horse Show at Houdain. We had entered for the best turned out Lorry and for several athletic events. Unfortunately our lorry was disqualified owing to a mistake on my part in sending a type of lorry (Stores) not eligible. She was judged, however, and gained second place on points. In the running events Leading Mechanic Black won the 100 yards; D'Albiac, Black, Peachey, and Brownridge won the 220 yards Relay; Lynn and James were 2nd in the three-Legged Race, and I got home 3rd in the Quarter Mile.

On June 23rd we had McAllister killed in a crash. He had been on an offensive patrol with his Flight, and when over Neuville St. Vaast on the way home, his machine broke in the air whilst he was doing a practice spin.

On the 25th we had a visit from the Prince of Siam, and in the afternoon I went to the

First Army Horse Show with D'Albiac and ran in the quarter-mile.

Little put up a good show for our benefit on the 26th. Through our telescope on the aerodrome we saw an Aviatick approaching from the *Vimy Ridge* direction and off went Little to deal with him. The report of the fight from an independent source was as follows :—

"One Sopwith triplane engaged one enemy machine over the line Vimy-Oppy. The enemy came to ground about one mile behind Acheville out of control. One man fell from machine while fighting. Triplane had the advantage all through the fight."

Judged from the standpoint of actual flying, Little was just an average sort of pilot with tremendous bravery and a flair for finding his way about. There was nothing particularly accurate or finished about his flying, but for getting the last ounce out of an aeroplane as an offensive weapon, he had few equals. Air fighting seemed to him to be just a gloriously exhilarating sport, and he had been doing regular work over the lines for many months before I can remember his showing any sign of fatigue or nervous strain. When out on a job of work he never ceased to look for trouble, and very little escaped those keen eyes of his. In combat, his dashing methods, close range fire and deadly aim made him a formidable opponent, and he was the most chivalrous of warriors. As a man, he was a most lovable character, and a sportsman in the truest sense of the word. When not flying his greatest joy was to go out after rabbits or rats with those other two great sportsmen, our fox terriers "Maurice" and "Tich," who adored him.

Booker and I went on leave on June 26th and whilst at Dover on the way back on July 7th, I saw something of the big Gotha raid on London. One effect of this raid was to prolong our stay at St. Eloi, for which we were profoundly thankful. There had been a proposal to transfer us to the 14th Wing on the Belgian coast, but the Gotha raid put the wind up people at home to such an extent that the Military Authorities were forced to withdraw squadrons from France to defend London. No. 45 Squadron was taken from our Brigade, and as this left only two Fighter Squadrons (No. 40 and ourselves) our move was cancelled.

Early in July we started to change our triplanes for Sopwith "Camels," and the note in the Squadron Diary for the 10th of July that Arnold, Johnston, and Knight flew "Dixie," "Veda" and "Peter III." to Dunkirk will recall some of the names we had for machines in those days. "The Frivolities" entertained the Ship's Company that night. We were still very Naval, you see.

It had been a hot summer so far and this had encouraged us to dig a swimming bath. I cannot remember whose brainwave this was, but it proved a huge success. In our spare time, too, we had been playing quite a lot of cricket, and early in August we organised a riding school. One, Captain Stadward, used to send up half-a-dozen horses and a Sergeant Major from his Camp close by whenever we had a spare afternoon, and D'Albiac, Booker, Johnston, Jenner-Parson, Thompson, Thornley, Scott, and myself used to place ourselves at the mercy of the S.M. and have the greatest fun. Who can ever forget "Cross your stirrups— ter-r-r-ot"!

The weather was consistently bad from July 24th to August 11th, and the only matters of general interest recorded in the Diary were a couple of Inter-Flight Football Matches, some athletic sports at Aubigny at which Jenner-Parson won the Officers' 100 yards, and a note against August 1st that D'Albiac bought three pigs in Lillers for 60 francs each.

A number of changes had been taking place round about this time. Arnold, Compston, and Soar had left, C. P. O. Scott was promoted to W.O., and new arrivals were Munday, Davidson, Reid, Cooper, and Fowler.

On August 17th we lost two of our best fellows in a most unlucky way. A patrol of seven Camels went off at half-past-five in the evening and during a dog-fight with a bunch of Albatross Scouts near Lens, Johnston and Bennetts collided in the air and both were killed.

On September 6th D'Albiac left the Squadron to relieve Wing Commander Chambers as R.N.A.S. Liaison Officer at H.Q. R.F.C., and this brings me nearly to the end of my part of No. 8's story. Before Draper takes over this narrative as my successor, I must not forget the night flying attacks against balloon sheds and troops in which he and Munday distinguished themselves so greatly. The first attack of this sort was on the night of the 29th September; R.F.C. Communiqué No. 109 described it thus :

"Flight-Commander Munday, Naval Squadron No. 8, left the ground at about 9.45 p.m. and proceeded to attack a German Balloon Shed between Brebieres and Quiery-la-Motte. On finding the objective he dived down to within twenty feet of the ground and fired fifty rounds from each gun into the shed, which burst into flames. Flight-Commander Draper, when over Douai, saw the shed burning furiously so flew towards it and dived down, attacking the men who had gathered round in order to extinguish the fire. There is little doubt that the shed contained a balloon."

My time with the Squadron came to an end on October 27th, 1917, when I handed over to Flight-Commander Draper, and returned to England and my old Command, Guston Road Air Station, Dover. The Squadron gave a farewell party on the 25th, with a special Dinner Menu and Sing-Song Programme. I will always recall memories of a marvellously cheery evening.

And so ends my Chapter. One is left with the feeling of having done little justice to the subject, but if, in this brief *resumé* of the Squadron's first year in France, one has succeeded in recapturing some of the atmosphere and spirit of those days, something will have been accomplished, and perhaps individual memories of persons and events will serve to fill the gaps that are left.

CHAPTER II.

THE SECOND HALF OF THE WAR

By Major C. Draper, D.S.C.
(Squadron Commander R.N. with No. 8 Squadron R.N.A.S.)

CHAPTER II.

The Second Half of the War

When after a brief rest at Eastchurch in the summer of 1917, I returned to Dunkirk and reported to Captain Lambe, he said: "I'm sending you to No. 8 Squadron—it is my best Squadron. Bromet is in command and it will be a great opportunity for you, so look after yourself." After a few weeks as a Flight-Commander I very soon discovered how true his words were and what a name and reputation 8 Naval had, so I was as nervous as I was honoured when I took over from Bromet on the latter's promotion to Wing-Commander on 28th October, 1917. I found a marvellous *esprit de corps* and spirit in the Squadron, and the way we went from success to success is testimony of this. I cannot speak too warmly of the work of my predecessor.

Operations and Movements.

Just about this time we were specialising in "interference." A series of Compass Stations had been set up along our front, and by a special land line to our Telephone Exchange we got news of any hostile aircraft "spotting" for their guns immediately one started working, so we could send out a couple or more machines to try and "interfere" with the shoot, and if possible attack the machine. It must be borne in mind that to spot successfully for artillery a machine must keep in the locality all the time the guns are firing and send in observations regularly, so that a shoot is definitely upset if the spotting machine can even be driven away.

The reports I received from the Army showed that out of the Artillery Spotters reported to us in this way we were successful in stopping 85 per cent. In fact we were so successful at this that the R.F.C. Wing-Commander under whose orders we came for operations arrived one day and said: "Draper, I'm not going to give you any more of the usual daily operation orders for Patrols, you will have a free hand to operate exactly as you like." I think this one of the greatest compliments ever paid any Squadron.

We came in for lots of other special work, however, escorting our own bombers, low strafing, and bombing.

In January 1918 *seven* pilots were decorated. A tribute indeed.

We continued at Mont St. Eloi until the end of March, 1918, suffering only five casualties, which was remarkable considering the flying done. This had proved a particularly strenuous period for the Squadron, and it was a great relief when we were sent home on the 3rd March, 1918, for a badly needed rest. Naval 8 was the first complete Naval Squadron to be sent to co-operate with the R.F.C. in the Field, and with the exception of three weeks at Dunkirk in February, 1917, during re-equipment, it was in the thick of it the whole time. We flew our machines back to Walmer in Kent, the men coming over in a monitor. The quiet and peace of Walmer, and the charming old house we had for quarters, were in striking contrast to active service conditions. Two-thirds of the Squadron went on leave immediately and it was a bitter blow to all when they had to be re-called most unexpectedly before the end of the month. But the Hun had started his big Spring Offensive and we were wanted urgently, so back we flew to Teteghem for a couple of nights, and then on to the never-to-be-forgotten La Gorgue and back with the same R.F.C. Wing and Brigade as before. But, oh! What a change. I always look on that trip to Walmer as the beginning of the end, and I don't think the Squadron was ever quite the same again, though we almost got into our old form at Serny.

On the 1st April, 1918, when the R.F.C. and R.N.A.S. were amalgamated, the Royal Air Force was established and we lost our naval status and became No. 208 R.A.F. I know everyone from myself down to the last man were very upset at the change. After being "borne on the books" of H.M. Ships for so long it was impossible suddenly to switch over from the Naval Ranks, Ratings and Routine we loved so much to those of the Army adopted by the R.A.F., which we didn't like. We seemed to lose that special distinction which had earned for Naval 8 a reputation second to none and which enabled it to accomplish so much. I don't mind admitting now that I made the fullest use of the unique position we were in before this amalgamation by pleading "Urgent R.F.C. requirements" when I wanted any machines or stores from H.Q. at Dunkirk, and by reversing the tactics and keeping the R.F.C. staff well in their place if they tried any "funny business" with the executive or administrative side of the Squadron. Unofficially we never dropped the old ways completely. A photograph taken after the Armistice on the day before I said good-bye to the Squadron displays at least two of us clinging tenaciously to the old uniform. It was terribly hard getting used to Majors, Captains, Sergeants, etc., but gradually as new drafts and pilots from R.A.F. depôts, who had never known either the R.F.C. or R.N.A.S., came along we accustomed ourselves to new ways. I well remember, however, insisting on my servant and driver, Welch and Tame, also on the Wardroom Staff, sending home for their blue Naval uniforms, and on all special occasions we all three wore the old R.N.A.S. uniform to the last.

The tragedy of La Gorgue occurred only seven days after our arrival there. The aerodrome was only about three and a half miles from the front which at that time was held by our Portuguese Allies. I cannot do better than include at this point my official report which is an exact copy of the one I sent to the O.C. 10th Wing at the time:—

No. 208 SQUADRON,
ROYAL AIR FORCE,
In the Field.
10th April, 1918.

"THE OFFICER COMMANDING,
10th Wing, R.A.F.

"Sir,—

"With reference to the destruction of the 16 machines of this Squadron I have the honour to submit the following report.

"About 4.00 a.m. on the morning of the 9th we were aroused by the sound of very heavy gun fire which increased in intensity towards dawn. There was considerable hostile shelling of MERVILLE and LA GORGUE and the surrounding districts. A large number of French civilians were passing west through our Camp, followed by considerable quantities of Portuguese Troops in open disorder without either rifles or equipment and apparently unofficered. By about 7 o'clock the shelling became very intense, but owing to the fog it was practically impossible to ascertain definitely where the shells were falling. I gave orders to have the machines removed from the hangars and spread out over the Aerodrome in case of a concentrated shelling of the hangars. I gave orders to Officers and men to pack all gear and stores as quickly as possible. As far as I remember, it was between 8 and 9 o'clock when I ordered officers, officers' stewards and as much mess gear as possible to leave officers' quarters without delay.

A shell had fallen in the farmhouse immediately alongside these quarters but it was impossible to tell whether the quarters were being deliberately shelled. A considerable quantity of shrapnel was falling all round. Several officers had very narrow escapes and an English sergeant from one of the local units was wounded in the face. He was sent to the sick bay on the Aerodrome for treatment. On my way over to the Aerodrome by car I was several times stopped by Portuguese officers imploring me to give them a lift, though I could not understand what they said. By this time only soldiers were falling back. I received a verbal message from a R.F.C. cyclist, through one of my officers, that the enemy had advanced and were in LAVENTIE. I got in telephonic communication with XV Corps Headquarters, being the only line left intact, and was informed by an officer of the Intelligence Branch that the enemy had attacked the Division on our right and on the whole of the Portuguese Front, and was coming forward. I reported the message I had received from the R.F.C. orderly, re LAVENTIE, but they could not confirm it. I then sent a despatch rider as far up to the line as he could get, but he returned, reporting that he spoke to three British officers east of LA GORGUE who informed him that the enemy had taken LAVENTIE and were just east of ESTAIRES. XV Corps were unable to confirm this, but I told them I was preparing to evacuate the Aerodrome. G.O.C. XV Corps asked me if I could carry out a reconnaissance, but I had to definitely refuse, it being impossible to see across the Aerodrome through the fog. The General did not wish me to leave LA GORGUE, but said if it was to save the machines from shell fire we could fly them away. I replied it was quite impossible to fly at all. I told him that I should act on my own as it was probable that the line would go at any moment. They intimated that this was possible as their other lines were down. I sent a second despatch rider up to the front, but he could not get through LA GORGUE village and returned without information.

"As far as I could judge, practically all our guns had been captured, as they were not firing at all. On the other hand the enemy artillery became increasingly active immediately in the vicinity of the Aerodrome. I think they were endeavouring to shell the railway and bridge immediately to the south of the Aerodrome.

"After careful deliberation with my Flight-Commanders I decided that I was not justified in risking personnel by flying away in the fog, though the majority volunteered to try. We then collected the machines in one bunch in the middle of the Aerodrome, the idea being for everyone to clear out and leave one officer with a cycle and side-car to stand by until the last moment with orders to destroy the machines if necessary. I was unable to get in touch with XV Corps so I ordered the telephone exchange and compass station to pack up. A British officer in a lorry which pulled up at the Aerodrome asked to borrow a car as he wanted to way-lay an ammunition supply column which was apparently coming up to LA GORGUE. I was unable to help him as I had sent the convoy off to SERNY. He informed me he was unable to get into LA GORGUE owing to the machine-gun fire. I then decided to burn the machines and retire from the Camp; as far as I can remember it was about 11 o'clock. The fog was as thick as ever and it was quite impossible to fly. I fully realised the seriousness of the situation but, being unable to communicate with any reliable authority, I had to act on my own. If there had been British troops in the area I should have left the machines for them to destroy, in accordance with orders, but I felt it extremely improbable that a panic-stricken crowd of Portuguese troops retiring in open disorder without equipment or officers would carry out this, even if they had received orders to do so. The ammunition supply column which had been parked on the road alongside the hangars had gone, their guns having been captured. The machines were then burnt and everyone cleared out by 11.30.

"I have described the events as nearly as possible in the order in which they occurred. The times I have given are only approximate. The only thing left behind was one Austin lighting set and some petrol and oil. The

Squadron packed and moved in under three hours.
       "I have the honour to be, Sir,
                Your obedient Servant,
                        (Sgd.)   C. Draper,
                                        Major."

It was some decision to have to take and was only taken after much consideration and consultation with my senior officers. There were many ready to try and fly, but being unable to ascertain the extent of the fog I felt personnel more valuable than machines.

We were then sent back to the large aerodrome at Serny to re-form and get new machines, and it says a good deal for the supply depôts that we got our full complement of over twenty machines in 48 hours.

There were three other squadrons at Serny, one of the largest aerodromes at the front, Nos. 18, 22 and 103, and very soon we were hard at work with them. We were nearly five months here and had a total of 103 combats, accounting for 86 of the enemy, with only six casualties of our own, and after the La Gorgue disaster it was a tremendous encouragement to receive the following letter from our old Skipper, Captain Lambe, at this time a Vice-Brigadier or something :—

                                22nd April, 1918.
"Dear Draper,
     "Hearty congratulations to you and the Squadron on the success of yesterday. I hope you will keep it up.
     "I am so glad that the Squadron is doing so well.
                Yours sincerely,
                        (Sgd.)   C. L. Lambe."

On the 26th August we carried out a special "strafe," making 42 flights over the enemy lines involving 38 hours 10 minutes flying. We dropped 153 20-lb. bombs and fired 5,400 rounds at enemy batteries and machine gun emplacements from very low altitudes.

We had almost recovered our old St. Eloi form, so it was a great disappointment to be most unexpectedly ordered south to Tramecourt, especially as the place had not previously been used as an aerodrome, and we had all the work of making it in addition to our work in the air, which could not be relaxed at all. During our two months' stay there we were much excited by the presence of His Majesty the King, who was staying in a château near by. I well remember the secrecy of his whereabouts. In spite of being the only one in the Squadron who was supposed to know I believe the news was round the Mess Decks before I got it. Being the nearest Squadron, I had special "most confidential" instructions to watch for enemy aircraft and got in a fierce panic when some hostile night bombers dropped half-a-dozen bombs in the vicinity, but I heard next day that the King had gone three days previously, and all was well.

Night bombing was now becoming very intensive on both sides, and a damn nuisance it was, keeping us out of bed half the night, especially as we could do nothing to help the situation.

Tramecourt was a small aerodrome on a decided slope and landing was most tricky. All will remember the pilot who removed the top of a tree and the corner of a Bessonneau Hangar and ended up in the hedge without hurting himself. It was at Tramecourt that I was sent my first N.C.O. Pilot, who I am sorry to say did not last very long, for apparently he got lost in the air and was last seen flying east into enemy country. We never heard of him again. No doubt this sounds incredible to the uninitiated, but it was astounding the number of new pilots who were lost in this way. Only those with actual experience knew how easy this was, and watching the new pilot was a Flight-Commander's greatest anxiety.

We left Tramecourt and the 10th Wing, with which the Squadron had been for sixteen months, on the 29th September, 1918, for the 22nd Wing and went to Foucacourt, right on the Somme. After the green fields and trees of the unspoiled area around Tramecourt, the desolation of the Somme was a terrific contrast. The Hun having started to retreat, we were advancing over the most blasted, barren and shell-ridden country imaginable; the so-called aerodromes were just old battle fields with the shell holes filled in, and for miles there wasn't a tree or building other than an Army hut.

From Foucacourt we moved on the 10th October forward to Estree for only seventeen days. I had a small personal adventure just about this time, when I was slightly wounded on the ground. This was somewhat amusing, after having been in the air at the front almost continuously since August 1916. I had motored up to the front to inspect an aerodrome that had just come into our hands, to see if it was fit to land on; I had with me a Staff Officer of the Brigade, and the Hun was shelling an ammunition dump near by while we were inspecting the ground, which appeared to be O.K., but just after we had taken our seats in the car a shell landed in the road behind and one piece of it knocked the driver's steel helmet off, and another hit me on the knee. I said: "I'm hit," but the Staff Officer only laughed and told me not to joke about these things. I said: "I'm not joking, it's quite true," and pulling up my coat I found I had quite a nice flow of blood, but it wasn't serious and I only laid up for a few days without leaving the Squadron. I had to pass a C.C.S. for the usual injection and duly appeared in the casualty list, so had to send a cable home to reassure my family.

For the next advance from Estree to Moritz on the 22nd October we had received special transport orders with a time table for our movements giving us two days for the move, which meant staying a night on the road somewhere. As the pilots could fly their machines on in an hour, and would have no food or sleeping accommodation on arrival, I thought I could improve on these instructions and got the Squadron through in the 24 hours. I was just patting myself on the back when the Wing-Commander arrived with the General, and I was throughly strafed for daring to imagine I could improve on the Brigade Staff work. I tried to tell myself that there must be some reason for the strange orders that come from such quarters, but any more inconsiderate bit of staff work could not be imagined.

Armistice Day will never be forgotten. The 'phone, which I always had by my bed, rang about 6.30 a.m. and the Wing-Commander himself said the Armistice would be signed at 11 a.m. and he wanted us to do a "Line Patrol" at 10 a.m., keeping well on our side and not being offensive in any way. And so it all ended. We managed to celebrate the event there and then and believe me there were no half measures. I have read and heard much of the celebrations at home but they simply couldn't equal those on the spot, although we hadn't quite the same facilities.

I took the Squadron forward on the 2nd December to Donstiennes, which was just south of the Belgian town of Charleroi. This of course was in the unstrafed part of the country and very comfortable we were after the Somme. We did very little flying and everyone was impatient to get home. I was relieved by Major Smart and said good-bye in January 1919.

Before going into details of the personnel of the Squadron, etc., I should like to put on record one of many instances which showed a certain human touch between the enemy and ourselves. On the 4th September, 1917, the Hun dropped a message almost on the aerodrome at St. Eloi which was typed and read as follows :—

"To the British Flying Corps—

"The Squadron of the part of Vimy is politely begged to give news of the observer and of the pilots, who are landed near Willerval the 5 of August.

"Are they dead or not? Thanking before.

The German Flying Corps."

This is an exact copy of the message, word for word, which I still have in my possession, but is only one of many that were dropped by both sides giving news of missing pilots.

My Flight Commanders.

Though several Leaders who had distinguished themselves and are mentioned by Bromet in the preceding chapter left for well-deserved rests or promotion about the time I took over, the Flight Commanders I was left with were about the ablest one could wish for.

The success of a Squadron in the air depended first and foremost on its Flight-Commanders, and Compston, who had " B " Flight, was a wonderful example. He was one of the most remarkable men at the front, and because of his youth, frail nature and highly strung temperament I was always anxious about him. Though he suffered greatly from neuralgia and loss of sleep, caused no doubt by the ever-increasing high altitudes at which we had to work, he had indomitable courage and nothing held him back. Although this was his second long spell at the front, it was not until the whole Squadron went home in March 1918 that I could persuade him to give up and take the rest he so richly deserved. He joined the Squadron when it was originally formed in October 1916 and except for one break of six weeks in 1917 was fighting in the air the whole time. His air tactics were worked out to the highest degree and he holds the unique distinction of never having lost a pilot over the lines. To read his own chapter on " The Flight Commander " is to appreciate how difficult this was. He had already been awarded the D.S.C. and bar during Bromet's time, and more than earned the second bar and D.F.C. while with me.

The loss in February 1918 of Price, who led " C " Flight, was a great blow. Everyone will remember this staunch, strong and silent Irishman, and the Captain Kettle beard he grew : he was a most daring and fearless officer and it seemed a terrible sacrifice to lose him in one of those low flying stunts that H.Q. were then serving out with increasing frequency. He was awarded the D.S.C. on the 1st January, 1918.

I then lost Macdonald in the same way in May, 1918. A fine big-hearted Canadian whom the Squadron could ill afford to spare.

The one with me longest was Jordan, who was a Flight-Lieutenant in the Squadron when I joined and was Flight-Commander from April to August, 1918. In December, 1917, he was awarded the D.S.C., a Bar to it within three weeks, and the D.F.C. in July, 1918. He was a remarkable fellow, thin and pale, and here was another who had simply to be forced to go home for a rest. He had joined up originally as an air mechanic, so he knew how to get the best out of his men. No Squadron Commander could

FURNES

MONT St. ELOI

The Aerodrome at Mont St. Eloi from the Air

wish for a more reliable Flight-Commander and when I heard of his death in a motor accident some years after the war I knew I had lost a staunch supporter and friend. Though to some he may have at times appeared hard and bitter he was at heart generous and sincere. I recall with amusement how some years later he told me that he thought I was much too lenient in those days with both officers and men and after a time he ceased to report any of his men to me because I always let them off.

Other Flight Commanders who distinguished themselves during my command were awarded decorations as follows : —

R. B. Munday—D.S.C. and Belgian Croix
de Guerre.
J. B. White (a Canadian)—D.F.C.
W. E. G. Mann—D.F.C.
A. Story—D.F.C.

MY PILOTS.

Space forbids a detailed account of everyone, though I could write a chapter about each of them. To me it was a very sad thing to add the name of Walworth to the Roll of Honour, because of the circumstances in which he was posted to 8 Naval and the personal relationship between my own family and his. When home on leave at Christmas 1917 and dining with my family at the Adelphi Hotel, Liverpool, young Walworth, in the uniform of a Sub-Lieutenant R.N.A.S., was dining with his family at the next table. He told me he had just passed out of the

Flying School and was posted to Dunkirk. His father asked me to try and get him to my Squadron, which was very easily done, and we were duly joined by this young golden-haired blue-eyed child, who looked about 16. I never met anyone so keen and literally bubbling over with enthusiasm. His letters home to relatives and friends, which at times it was my duty to censor, were a fine example of British spirit. I remember one particular letter just after he got back from a scrap with bullet holes in the petrol tank, and his machine generally shot about; it was a letter to a school friend and he said: "I've just landed back with holes in my petrol tank, but you simply don't know or feel the danger, it's just one big thrill, hurry up and come out, it's just wonderful." He only lasted a couple of months, poor boy, and was shot down in flames on our side of the line. In my letter home to his people I particularly avoided any reference to the way he met his death, so it was more than distressing for them when some tactless infantry officer who reached the wreckage first took his cigarette case and pocket book, which were of course badly charred, and sent them direct to his father.

The twelve casualties I had during my time were very few in number, considering all things, but each one was a personal loss, as I cannot think of a unit more united or more of a big happy family. We appreciated each other as only men can under those conditions and I never heard one quarrel or one unkind word the whole time, nor was any man prouder of them than I was. The results we got were due in no small measure to this comradeship. "Greater love hath no man than this, that he lay down his life for his friend," and I can truthfully say that everyone in the Squadron was ready to do this.

OTHER OFFICERS.

On my Ground Staff I counted myself more than lucky to get Pinkney. I had known him at Eastchurch and when I heard he was to be posted overseas I at once asked Dunkirk for him, as I had a vacancy for an Armament Officer.

Quite early in his training at home he had realised the obvious truth that to be of practical help to pilots and to be able to appreciate their gunnery difficulties an Armament Officer should be a pilot himself and in spite of much opposition by the Authorities at home he took his Pilot's certificate. Though it was never officially recognised and he was never allowed to be an active service pilot, this experience made him invaluable. As he had originally applied to be a pilot and was turned down on account of eyesight, I had the greater admiration for his determination. He joined at the same time as I took over from Bromet and until he went home in July, 1918, was officially our Armament Officer, but actually he was much more than this, for he became the "Father" and friend of us all. His loyalty and support, his never-failing cheerfulness under all conditions meant much to me, and when we left St. Eloi he not only shared my hut, but shared my troubles and difficulties. Being several years my senior in age, I found his counsel and advice of tremendous help, and saw at once what a wonderful influence he had in the Mess and how the pilots loved him and went to him with their troubles.

The efficiency of the Armament Branch under him was remarkable, nothing was too much trouble, as he worked unceasingly. Time and again I have known him stay up all night to solve some gun problems. I never heard one complaint from my pilots about this side of their work.

At one period both the Wing Medical Officer, Cranston, and the Brigade Chaplain, Keymer, made 8 Naval their H.Q. and lived with us. I took it as a great compliment when they asked if they might do so. All present will remember the night of St. Eloi when the Padre got up a very frank debate on certain matters and the very outspoken remarks of one Broach, one of the Canadian pilots. I only mention this to show how varied the social life in the Squadron was.

GENERAL.

I don't think any Squadron could have had more amusing side-lines than ours. We did everything, went everywhere and had an amazing number of "Guest Nights" or "Special Dinners" which were got up when anyone was promoted, decorated or leaving. Then visits from Generals, Wing Commanders, or other notabilities had to be properly honoured, and if we hadn't an excuse for a celebration we invented something. We went out to other Squadrons a great deal and got quite a name for our social activities and Concerts. We were the originators of the

Theatre which with the help of the other Squadrons was built in a hut at Serny. It had a proper stage, curtain and lighting. Any sort of diversion was jumped at and we got as far afield in tenders as Boulogne, St. Pol, Amiens and even Paris. It was surprising not to have to record casualties in connection with one or two of these escapades.

Just after the Americans came into the war we had two or three officers of their Flying Corps and quite a number of their mechanics sent to us to study our methods and work at the front, so baseball and other new stunts were added. I think nearly every known card game was played at one time or the other; poker would be the craze for a while, then vingt-et-un and the well known game with two dice and the rude name was often played into the small hours.

The supply of food and drink was always a great anxiety, it being difficult to get much variety. Tenders had to be sent a long way to get anything fresh and at times they could ill be spared. A spell of bad weather relieved the pressure of work with the machines and was a welcome change on many occasions, since we usually managed to get a tender into Boulogne. Though the Army canteens did their best the demand on them was terrific and there was the usual scrounging. With regard to alcohol, and in spite of all that has been said and written lately, I say unhesitatingly that it played a big part. It would have been impossible to have had the hundreds of successful dinners and wonderful evenings we had without it, but no one who reads this or the history of any other squadron need think life was one long "orgy" or that we were carried to bed every night, because alcohol was damned hard to get, and what we did manage to obtain had to be nursed for special occasions. However, I don't think we were at any time actually "Dry" though occasionally our guests had some queer mixture for cocktails.

Amongst some of our distinguished visitors at St. Eloi was Sir Douglas Haig. He was on a tour of inspection of that part of the Front Line, and The G.O.C.'s A.D.C. being a personal friend had asked me to provide a hut for him and his staff to lunch in. We all felt duly honoured, but it put the wind up me because of the very severe Army orders forbidding cameras at the front, since I think Sir Douglas must have heard the ' clicks ' as he left the hut. I remember, too, visits from Sir John Simon, Prince Alex of Denmark and Mr. Winston Churchill, and just after the Armistice I had the honour of dining with the Prince of Wales at our Brigade H.Q.

My Men.

It is quite impossible to give enough praise to the fellows who comprised "the lower deck." To them was due the efficiency of the machines, engines, guns, transport, workshops, stores, office, telephones and the day and night routine that kept up the supplies of food, cooking and the enormous amount of work that had to be done to keep pilots and machines in the air. No other branch of the fighting forces required so many specialists—mechanics, carpenters, armourers, chauffeurs, blacksmiths, clerks, cooks, and so on, and no other Squadron had a finer set of these than 8 Naval, not necessarily all experts, but *workers*. Without these we could have done nothing. There is no doubt that the Admiralty attracted the best type, and the superiority of the Naval Squadrons, particularly Naval 8, over the R.F.C. Squadrons was largely due to the rank and file. It was remarkable how little trouble they were and I knew of their hardships, too. Though discipline had to be maintained, "Defaulters" were few and far between and during the 17 months of my command I cannot remember one serious case. The main object was keeping pilots fit and machines in the air, and when by mutual trust, understanding and co-operation of officers and men this was done, anything became possible. We got the best out of them by realising the simple truth that they hated the war as much as the rest of us and were as anxious to get on with it as we were. Like all other Units, there were never enough men for the dozens of extra working parties continually required, especially if the Flights had more than one machine under repair; but let me say in conclusion, that no C.O. had his task made lighter than by the loyal support these men gave me.

The Machines.

The Sopwith Camels, 130 h.p. Clerget engine, with two machine guns, which were just replacing the Triplanes when I took over, were a big advance on the latter, and being pretty new on the front, were a great help. They gave us new life, and nothing encourages a pilot so much as confidence in his machine. Our superiority over the enemy did not last very long, however, as the Hun soon came out with something new, but we again got "on top" when still newer Camels with 150 h.p. Bentley engines came through in February, 1918. About this time the fitting of small bomb racks under the fuselage to carry four 20-lb. bombs irritated us a good deal. The machines were designed purely as single seater fighters and the extra weight made a big difference to the performance when every ounce and every second might mean a life saved. Also, proper sights for bomb dropping could not be fitted to these "fighters," but Pinkney worked out an expedient whereby approximate lines of sight could be taken by looking over the side of the fuselage.

As I have told earlier, these Bentley Camels were lost at La Gorgue, so we felt badly let down when we were re-equipped from an R.F.C. supply base with the old Clerget Camel. I never ascertained why, but up to the formation of the R.A.F., the Naval machines supplied us from Dunkirk were in finish, workmanship and performance superior to those supplied to the R.F.C. through the War Office. This was proved a hundred times in the air as we discovered for ourselves after the amalgamation.

Next to his guns, when in action a pilot's greatest anxiety in those days was his engine, and I fear that not many pilots knew anything about them. It was the exception to find one who did (Jordan was one of the few) since training at home was necessarily hurried. The Clerget was not solid enough and soon rattled itself to pieces. I got out a list of "Don'ts" for running Rotary Engines which makes amusing reading now :—

NAVAL SQUADRON No. 8.
13th November, 1917.

DON'T open up STRAIGHT AWAY, it does not give the oil a chance to circulate, and ruins the obdurators.

DON'T run your engine TOO LONG on the ground. It is only necessary to open up full for a FEW SECONDS.

DON'T forget to test BOTH magnetos when running on the ground, and occasionally in the air.

DON'T exceed 1,250 revolutions at any time. It causes the ball-races to "creep," and other unpleasant things.

DON'T allow your engine to "pop" or "bang." It is caused by TOO MUCH PETROL and damages the valves in addition to overheating.

DON'T "blip" except when throttled right down. It is extremely bad flying and puts unnecessary strain on the whole machine.

DON'T switch off at any time in the air or the plugs will oil up.

DON'T close the throttle when the petrol is turned off. Allow a cool draught to blow right through the engine by keeping it wide open.

DON'T miss a chance to let your engine cool down, by a short glide after a long stiff climb.

DON'T always set the control levers by the figures on the bracket, but by the SOUND of the engine. That ever-changing density of the air requires an ever-changing mixture.

DON'T forget there will be no pressure in the tank after a long glide with the engine off.

DON'T condemn an engine immediately you are "let down."

DON'T be too ready to blame your mechanics.

DON'T forget that SYMPATHY and a thorough knowledge of all "work," especially "carburation," is very important.

DON'T forget the oil pulsator.

While at Serny we conceived the idea of making one of our Camels into a two-seater, as the Hun was well "on top" of us at the moment and it was difficult to keep off attacks from the rear, and a gunner able to fire behind would do this and surprise the Hun, who would not expect scouts to be so armed. By a little "wangle" I managed to get an extra machine and we altered it ourselves on the spot, even to making a new and smaller tank, and though it flew quite well and up to our expectations, in spite of somewhat amateurish calculations on paper, when the Authorities discovered it we got severely strafed and ordered to re-convert it immediately, although we did have a chance to take it over the lines. So much for that bit of enterprise!

The last new machine we got was the Sopwith Snipe with a 200 h.p. Bentley engine. These came through to us at Foucacourt on the Somme in October, 1918, and were England's last word in Fighting Scouts, but the Armistice came so soon afterwards that we never had a real chance of using them against the enemy, who was retreating so fast that hostile aircraft were few and far between.

This brings my chapter to its conclusion, but I must add, and ask all those who read to bear in mind, that it has been written chiefly from memory, thirteen years since these things happened. There are bound to be omissions, many names left out, and many incidents unrecorded. The period under review was just "cram full" from first to last, and for me it was the greatest period of my life. Though the War affected all young men in diverse ways and left its tragic mark on so many, I wouldn't have missed it for a chance to live my life again, and every detail of those days and the memory of the friends I made will ever be my dearest recollections.

CHAPTER III.

THE FLIGHT-COMMANDER

By Squadron-Leader R. J. O. Compston, D.S.C., D.F.C.

(Flight-Commander R.N. with No. 8 Squadron R.N.A.S.)

CHAPTER III.

The Flight Commander

A pilot, even though he were a superb flier, did not necessarily become a successful Flight-Commander, and I have known many Flight-Commanders who, by no stretch of the imagination, could be called good pilots, but whose leadership was of a high order.

Initiative, clear sight, navigating ability, the power to impart knowledge and balanced judgment are some of the main attributes which made the successful Flight-Commander in the Great War.

Number 8 Squadron, Royal Naval Air Service, later known as "Naval 8"—a name which was given to it by the Royal Flying Corps pilots of the squadrons with which it worked—and known now in the Royal Air Force as Number 208

Squadron—was singularly fortunate in starting its career with several men who were born leaders. To these men many of us owe not only our gratitude, but everything we possess, for, had it not been for their care and foresight, their skill in adapting themselves to strange conditions and their initiative, we would not in our turn have been able to lead flights and pass on the knowledge they gave us. Such a man was Colin Roy Mackenzie, my Flight Commander when the Squadron went down to work with the Royal Flying Corps on the Somme front in 1916.

At that time we knew little about aerial fighting, for the area where we had been (Nieuport, Ostend and Dunkirk) was amply defended by anti-aircraft guns. Unlike some of our Allies, the Germans believed in manning their anti-aircraft guns with some of their finest gunners, and I for one certainly take off my hat to them for their shooting.

Our scanty knowledge of aerial fighting was soon augmented by bitter experience; the enemy were employing a great number of aeroplanes of every description on this front in 1916, and Mackenzie led us magnificently through those hectic days when we hardly knew what we were doing. I remember how he told us that when we were having a fight with another aeroplane we must bear in mind that there were two very frightened men in the picture, but the other man was the more frightened of the two. What excellent advice! For surely, if one could truly believe this, a battle was half won before the start. I could write much of these early days of the Squadron, of the escapes we had, of Mackenzie's warnings to us when we were about to be picked off by enemy scouts, but I must resist this temptation, or the limited space at my disposal will be exhausted long before I have touched on all I wish. The Squadron suffered a great blow when Mackenzie failed to return one day after an offensive patrol, and we heard from the enemy, after I had dropped a message over the lines asking for information, that he had crashed fatally and was buried with full military honours. So passed a born leader and a brave man.

Another man who had outstanding claims to recognition was Little, who, unlike Mackenzie, was not so much a leader as a brilliant lone hand. I feel safe in saying that there have been few better shots, either in the Services or outside, than this man. I have seen him bring down a crow on the wing with a .22 rifle and break bottles thrown into the air while they were still travelling upward; what more deadly foe could be found than such a man, armed with two machine guns firing at the rate of 2,000 rounds per minute? Once Little came within range of an enemy he did not give up until (1) the enemy was shot down, (2) his own engine failed, or (3) he ran out of ammunition. He had in human guise the fighting tendencies of a bull dog—he never let go. Small in stature, keen-eyed, with face set grimly, he seemed the epitome of deadliness; sitting aloft with the eyes of a hawk he dealt death with unfailing precision. Seldom did he return to the aerodrome reporting an indecisive combat, for as long as petrol and ammunition held out, Little held on until the enemy's machine either broke up or burst into flames.

On one occasion this pilot dived with such persistence on his enemy that he forced the machine to land on our side of the lines. Killed while night flying against the enemy's Gothas, the country lost one who gained many honours for himself and his Squadron, a very gallant fighter with the courage of a lion.

Determination, pluck and the power to lead were the attributes of Price. Irish and impetuous, he gave much trouble to the enemy for, like Little, he never gave in. Scorning the Aldis telescopic sight for his guns, he would put his head over the side of the machine and watch his tracer bullets riddling the enemy; this gave him no small amount of satisfaction and I can see the sparkle in his eyes as he said to me one day: "Sure I drilled him like a cullender till the blighter burst into flames." We presume he was killed while shooting down an enemy kite balloon and no doubt he was looking over the side watching his tracer bullets go into it when a bullet hit him in the head, so he died with the sparkle in his eyes, engine roaring, guns spurting flame in glorious action. Had he been told his time must come, he would have asked for nothing better than to die like this.

Jordan would be rightly described as a scientific fighter; he combined dash and courage with sound common sense; his heart was in the right place, but he never allowed it to overrule his head. He realised, as others before him, that a Flight-Commander's duty was (1) to get into active touch with the enemy to their detriment and (2) to preserve the lives of the pilots under his leadership. Such statement may call forth the remark that I am labouring the obvious, but if so I beg to differ, and for this reason—by weighing the pros and cons of a prospective fight before engaging the enemy, lives were sometimes retained which might otherwise have been lost. It was my privilege to instruct this officer in aerial fighting, and for many months he flew with me as my right hand man, learning my methods, gaining confidence and shooting down the enemy until he was appointed to lead the flight in which he was fledged and "blooded." Rather a silent man, but with a charm all his own. No one ever knew why Jordan, when in a jovial post-prandial mood, imagined he was captain of a ship and insisted on walking the quarter-deck. So harmless a pastime could cause no offence if the room were clear, but it seldom was, and woe betide those who got in his path, for he simply walked straight through them. On these occasions he wore his hat at the "Beatty" angle, a set expression on his fine ascetic face, and his hands behind his back— truly a man of character even when enjoying "superelevation." He was spared during hostilities but met a tragic end in a motor accident after the war. On those who knew him well he left his mark. A man of exceptional charm, although reserved, he gave his friendship to few, but those of us who had it valued it highly.

Talking of reserve turns my mind at once to Booker, a man who said remarkably little but who did much; he was a tiger for fighting—nor was this spirit directed only against the enemy—for he fought for his own men to get what he wanted for them. I remember on one occasion he thought I had got an extra aeroplane which he should have had, and the amount of energy he put into the verbal fight would have surprised even the Socialist back benchers; personally, I admired him for it, he knew what he wanted and he just went out to get it. Jealously he guarded the rights of his men, fearlessly he preserved the lives of his pilots and bravely he attacked the enemy, until one day the odds against him were too numerous even for his skill and spirit, and so fell one who will ever have his place in the memory of his friends as a very sterling fighter.

Alas, these men have gone, but there remain with us many who merit equal praise, whose leadership was of just as high an order, whose skill and bravery have left as strong a mark on the records of achievement in the war. Much could be written concerning each one, and nothing would give me greater pleasure than the pleasant task of setting out their history and achievements, but lack of space precludes this,

Flight-Commander
R. J. O. COMPSTON,
D.S.C., R.N.

Flight-Commander
C. D. BOOKER,
D.S.C., R.N.

Flight-Commander
W. L. JORDAN,
D.S.C., R.N.

Flight-Commander
R. B. MUNDAY,
D.S.C., R.N.

and I must content myself with setting down the names of those who, as it were, formed the vertibræ of No. 8 Squadron, who earned for it so enviable a name, and who, in their respective spheres, are carrying on, bringing to their daily job the same spirit which animated us all in the Squadron—I refer to S. Q. Goble, A. R. Arnold, J. C. P. Wood and C. Draper. Each helped to make or maintain the traditions of the Squadron; each worked in his own way for its good, for the destruction of the enemy aircraft and for the preservation and training of his pilots.

Now before proceeding to describe the duties and work of a Flight-Commander, I must outline briefly the disposition of a Squadron. Commanded by a Squadron Commander there were three Flight-Commanders in charge of A, B, and C flights; each had five or six officers in his flight and a rigger and fitter to each aeroplane, of which there were six as a rule. In addition to the three fighting flights there was Headquarters flight consisting of workshops, records office and ground staff, etc. The work of the Squadron was decentralised, so that each Flight-Commander was responsible to the C.O. for the condition of his aeroplanes, the fitness of his pilots, and the welfare and efficiency of his men. It will be seen, therefore, that a Flight-Commander had plenty to keep him occupied when he was not in the air. For example, his aeroplanes had to be maintained in good condition, so that he could produce the maximum number at all times for duty. To do this necessitated close co-operation with the Chief Petty Officer in charge of the flight as to the best time to undertake repairs, etc., whether to allow a certain machine to fly a few more hours before overhaul or whether to work a night shift and have all ready for the morning. The fitness of his officers covers rather a lot. It was definitely a Flight-Commander's job to become well acquainted with each one of his pilots, to make friends of them and to help them in every possible way to pick up the threads of aerial warfare and to carry on perfecting themselves in their piloting (many officers came to France immediately after passing out of flying schools in England). To this end it was necessary to arrange gunnery practice and formation flying in addition to the lighter but nevertheless important side of keeping the body healthy by football matches, for a war pilot should be clear of eye and have the blood pulsating healthily through his veins if he is to bring all his energies and faculties to bear when facing the enemy in the air. Much could be gathered about the methods of aerial fighting by discussion, and it was part of a Flight-Commander's duty to see that his pilots gained all possible knowledge which could be imparted on the ground. An aerial combat discussed afterwards in comfort on the ground often revealed where a mistake had been made, and by such methods a flight could be brought to a high pitch of efficiency and developed into an invaluable fighting unit.

I should not like to proceed without first paying tribute to those who made it possible for us to leave the ground with confidence, for one of the essentials in successful single-seater fighting is confidence in the aeroplane, and one might truly say the morale of the Squadron depends largely on this. In No. 8 we had, without exception, the finest lot of men the Royal Naval Air Service could produce, drawn from every branch of trade, many of them ex-naval ratings. They all worked unsparingly to keep our machines in good condition. I say "unsparingly" advisedly, for the conditions under which they sometimes had to work were deplorable. Imagine nine inches of snow on the ground, with icy wind blowing through many holes in a canvas Bessoneaux Hangar, the feel of cold spanners and frozen oil, the making of delicate adjustments with hands numbed to the bone; thus would our men willingly work if any one of us had come back from patrol and complained that his engine seemed a little rough. I remember on one occasion I came back from patrol and said as I got out of the machine: "The engine is a bit rough and uneven, but I don't know what it is." My Chief Petty Officer replied: "Leave it to me, sir, and go in and get warm and rested." This happened after the last patrol of the day, and the next morning, when I went into the shed, I found that my engine had been completely dismantled and built up during the night; nothing much was found to be amiss, but when I tested it the roughness had certainly disappeared.

Truly did these men deserve our praise. With confidence did we trust them implicitly, knowing they realised that—although not spectacular

—their work was the foundation of all our hopes and victories, without them we could have achieved nothing. Our victories were their joys and our defeats their sorrows. Their selfless devotion to duty coupled with their skill and conscientious work have built up a monument for all time to the spirit of team work and co-operation.

Having set out briefly certain definite duties which devolved upon the Flight-Commander on the ground I want to describe something of his work in the air. First and foremost his duty was to bring down, drive down, or prevent from working all enemy aircraft in that sector of the front which his C.O. had ordered him to patrol, and at the same time to preserve the lives of his pilots. How easily written this last sentence, but how difficult of attainment was the preservation of those lives.

Bearing in mind the fact that there were no text books on aerial fighting, experience was hard gained in this new departure. To those who lost their lives in gaining this experience belongs much honour, for they learned and passed on to others the first elementary rules governing procedure in air warfare. Later in the War it was possible so to instruct a pilot on the ground that he went into the air behind his Flight-Commander with more chance of surviving than had his early pioneer brothers, for they followed blindly where their leader went, not realising what his plans were, and he might not have been able to give a very clear plan of action, as he had little time or opportunity to think things out. Flung suddenly into the air to lead others—someone had to—truly the life of an early Flight-Commander was not a picnic. At that time the enemy aeroplanes were not known by name, for none had been brought down on our side of the lines; we knew them as types, which we identified by silhouettes which had been drawn by various pilots; thus in our combat reports we would refer to an engagement with a type "K" or "C."

You may possibly have been wondering how a Flight-Commander in one small aeroplane could make known his orders to his other pilots in their separate machines. The days of wireless telephony were not yet, but in spite of the lack of this it was remarkable to what pitch of efficiency in manœuvring a flight could be brought by merely moving the aeroplane; for example, a turn to the right would be signalled by rocking the machine from side to side and then dropping a wing down to the right and commencing the turn. The pilots on the right of the leader would slow down their engines and pull their machines up, slowing them as much as possible, while the leader would fly round in a normal manner; those on the left who had to complete the outer and greater circle, would put their noses down and go as fast as possible to catch up; thus would a turn be made, and when all were on an even keel after the turn each pilot would close up to his original distance from his next man. Such a manœuvre came easily after practice but, to an inexperienced pilot, it was extremely difficult. I remember being told, shortly after my arrival in France, to go up and practice formation flying with a brother officer, but when we were both in the air it seemed impossible to get close together. So used were we to flying in left hand circles round the aerodrome at the flying school that we continued to follow each other at a distance of about a mile, nor during the whole flight did we get closer than this. It might amuse you to hear, but I do not think the editor would pass for publication, the remarks which were made to us when we landed; but I am glad I did not take the advice of one fairly senior officer, who suggested that I might find my wartime vocation as a lighthouse keeper or some such job where movement was neither required nor looked for and where judgment of distance was not imperative. But I diverge from my theme, which was to tell you how many aeroplanes there were in a flight. As a general rule six were used and the shape of the formation was a "V"—similar to that used by wild geese—but, instead of flying on a level with one another, each pilot would be slightly higher than the man in front, thus lessening the risk of collision and making for easier visibility. The formation of five or six was considered to be the most manœuvrable, although larger formations were used in other spheres of air work. Once I prevailed on my commanding officer to let me lead the whole Squadron (18 aeroplanes) over the lines and we solemnly set out in "V" formation; the result was really amusing. As we approached the lines I saw a few enemy machines underneath us, but rather too low for us to waste our height; I watched them for a while, and when they saw us, how they scuttled for home! We must have looked like a cloud of locusts. Of course, we defeated our own object, for every enemy machine we saw dived down to its aerodrome as soon as this cloud of British aeroplanes approached. I told the C.O. when we landed that a close parallel to what happened could be seen in the evening by walking suddenly into a forest glade full of rabbits feeding. I had hoped that we should be able to engage the famous Baron von Richtofen's Squadron, but the times of our patrols did not coincide, and of him more anon.

To return once more to the formation of a flight, it was my custom to put the newest arrivals in the flight as numbers four and five or five and six in the formation, because here they were higher than the other three of us and could watch everything which took place. I did my best not to lead them into any scrap where enemy aircraft would be above them, and from this comparatively safe altitude they quickly gained experience of aerial combats and what I call "air sight." Let me explain what I mean —it does not follow that because a man can see a figure a mile away on the ground and be able to see whether it be man or woman, that he will be able to see things in the air, for I have known many men with first class sight who, when they commenced aerial work, appeared to be quite blind at times; this was chiefly due to the fact that an inexperienced pilot had to give most of his attention to the leader, watching closely for signals; he therefore could not be expected to see as much as one whose eyes were attuned to distance and whose whole attention could be given to finding the enemy. I remember one of my pilots, seeing me fire at something (he did not see it was an enemy aeroplane, although we were very close to it), fired his guns —presumably in sympathy—hitting the middle plane of my Triplane about twelve inches from my right shoulder. The following incident also illustrates what I have said about "air sight." I was asked by one of the pilots in the Squadron if I would lead him to a position where he could see a real live enemy; he had done a number of patrols, but had not been in close contact with the enemy. We set out together and after gaining a good height (17,000 feet) I was fortunate enough to see an enemy two-seater coming from our own side of the lines. I say fortunate, because these aircraft were very difficult to engage, being capable of attaining great height and they were fast; in fact, in some instances I have known such machines to have been faster and better climbers than our own fighting scouts of the time. Experience told me that this machine had been over our lines for the purpose of taking photographs of our supply dumps, ammunition dumps, camps and aerodromes, etc., and it was therefore of paramount importance that the photos should not be developed and their information used against us by the enemy.

Although the enemy machine was about 1,000 feet above us when I first saw it, we managed by a series of dives and climbs, to arrive in a suitable position underneath and, pulling up vertically, I put up a stream of bullets through which the pilot had to fly. Having lost all my speed in the vertical climb I fell over on my back, but while falling I saw the enemy machine make a flat turn (without banking) and nearly hit my pilot. Steeper and steeper dived the stricken enemy, until his port wings came off and he crashed near Loos, where we collected the wreckage later. On arrival at our aerodrome the pilot told me that he saw nothing at all except the machine which nearly hit him; he neither saw it come nor did he know to what end it had dived past him. Incidentally, neither the pilot nor the observer of the German machine could have known what was happening, for the pilot was shot in the head and the observer in the heart.

Now I should like to narrate as clearly as possible the atmosphere in which we worked and I think a description of a dawn patrol would achieve this. On the occasion I am going to describe the job was in the Arras-Lens sector which meant patrolling in a triangle, the points of which were Arras-Lens-Douai.

We were, of course, muffled up to the eyes and wore fleece-lined thigh boots drawn up over a fleece or fur-lined Sidcot suit, a fur-lined helmet complete with chin guard and goggles with a strip of fur all round them. Any parts of bare skin left open to the air were well coated with whale oil to prevent frost bite. For our hands we found that an ordinary pair of thin silk gloves, if put on warm and then covered with the ordinary leather gauntlet gloves, retained enough heat for the whole patrol. It was essential that a start should be made with plenty of warmth inside the clothing, for such heat could be retained; but if one started cold it was impossible ever to generate sufficient heat from the body, and I remember once having to come down from 3,000 feet only, so frozen that I had only just power to land the machine. I was incapable of pressing the triggers of the guns and had to be helped out of the machine and carried away.

Emerging from the mess we got into our machines, tested the engines, waved away the chocks (wooden blocks put in front of the wheels to prevent the machine running away while being tested) and opened our engines out into the darkness. While gaining height we saw away on our starboard beam a dark mass, which we knew to be the town of Arras, while the silvery twisting thread straggling eastward showed us the River Scarpe. An occasional bursting shell and some Verey Lights betrayed the whereabouts of the lines, while a star shell threw into clear relief the chalky contour of the Hindenburg line. Rudely we disturbed that quiet hour before the dawn, seeming the only living things in a sleeping world, and that curious light which precedes the dawn showed us the earth below softly stippled as though an artist had worked through the night on the whole vast canvas of the earth, softening the sharp outline of cities and reducing railways, roads and fields to a blur.

A rosy glow to eastward heralded the approaching dawn and we were getting into a good position to fly back towards our own lines with the sun behind us and so surprise any unwary early birds of the enemy. But before going on to describe the rest of this patrol I want to make an attempt to convey a picture of a sunrise from the air. I have once or twice seen the sun rise twice on the same morning, once from 18,000 feet up and again after I had landed. To the fighting pilot the sun was a wonderful friend when it was in the right position, for when he could attack with it behind his back there was little likelihood of the enemy seeing his approach.

After that curious half light which preceded the dawn a rosy glow would fill the east and then a golden ball started rising from behind the mists, as though a giant unseen hand were gently pushing it from below; many-coloured rays shot out, licking up the mists and seemed to wake the earth, until one almost saw it throb and sparkle into life and all its contours rise clear through the haze of night, as the golden orb climbed still higher, until it stood revealed in all its perfect glory. And it would seem to say: "Behold, I give you day and life," and to the fighting pilot specially would it say: "Shelter in my radiance, for I will blind your enemies, but beware lest your enemies usurp your place, for needs must I smile on the attacker and the attacked."

At 18,000 feet and twelve miles over the
enemy lines we turned and I surveyed the space
to the westward for any signs of enemy activity.
I was rewarded, for away on our starboard I
saw four hostile aircraft, as yet below us but
gaining height, while on our port beam I saw
five of the enemy about the same height as the
others. Ahead of us and about on our own
level was a two-seater flaunting its black crosses
in the early morning sun. This had to be engaged first and we had to remember to keep an
eye on the others, for if they outclimbed us while
we attacked the two-seater we should have been
in a difficult position, as they were nine strong
to our five. We lost height gradually, so that
we could come up under the tail of the enemy,
and he did not see us coming, for the friendly
rays of the sun shielded us and in any case he
was probably looking towards the west and not
expecting attack from the east at that early
hour; in fact, when we were quite close I saw
the observer looking over the side but towards
the west. We pulled up until our sights were
filled with the aeroplane and then we fired, hold-
ing on until we thought we should crash, then
over on our back to avoid collision. As we came
on to an even keel I saw volumes of black smoke
pouring out of the machine followed by a sheet
of flame which seemed to stretch for forty feet
into the air. Then, charred and lifeless, it
plunged headlong to the earth.

Pulling up, we climbed hard to regain the
height we had lost. I saw them as we turned

and what I expected had happened; the formation of four machines had joined up with the other of five; we therefore had nine machines to tackle next. We had the satisfaction of knowing that we could outclimb the enemy and this, coupled with the fact that they were still to westward of us and would therefore have difficulty in seeing us, outweighed the disadvantage in numbers, for as long as we kept above the enemy we had little to fear. After a little while we set a course towards them and I was pleased to see they made no sign of having noticed us. It was obvious to me that they had not seen the fate of their compatriots in the two-seater. Possibly the sun hid us to much advantage, or they were not thoroughly awake at that early hour, for they seemed to have no idea of our proximity. Their machines were painted the most vivid colours—bright red with black lines down the fuselage, green with blue markings, while some were a blotch of colour on the camouflage principle. The moment arrived and, each choosing a machine to dive at, away we went, glueing our eyes to the Aldis sights and keeping our fingers on the triggers. My adversary seemed to rush towards me and rapidly his head became larger in the centre ring of my sight—I was tempted to fire, but held on until I thought I should crash into him, then pressing the triggers for a few seconds only I was forced to pull over on to my back to avoid hitting him. Very few rounds of ammunition are necessary when fired at point blank range, for the rate of fire from two synchronised guns firing through our propellers was 2,000 rounds per minute. Once more on an even keel I surveyed what had, a few minutes before, been a peaceful German patrol and I saw one going down in flames while another was spinning down, apparently out of control, for the pilot did not right the machine, even when he disappeared against the earth's surface, thousands of feet below us. The remaining six machines had dived away and were making for home as hard as they could. My own pilots had taken up their position (with the exception of one) and almost as I had finished counting them I saw in the distance a triplane flying east and a good deal lower than we were. I learned afterwards that the compass of this pilot, who was at that time a new arrival in the Squadron, was frozen up and he had not the slightest idea where he was. We put our noses down, did the equivalent of what the Americans call "stepping on the gas," and flying round in front of the pilot collected him into the formation, much to his joy. Forced as I was to fetch this man, I had lost height and had gone further over the lines than I intended at this point of the patrol; however, I had to make the best of it and altered course for home, as our petrol was getting low. Fortunately, our efforts had cleared the sector and we were unlikely to run into any enemy aircraft at a greater altitude than that at which we were flying. For a short time all went well, when suddenly the "wuff-wuff" of anti-aircraft shells bursting in front of us disturbed our peace of mind, for we were now at a height of only nine thousand feet and a good target. As the bursts were in front of us we altered course to starboard and increased speed at the same time. The next bursts were on our port beam and not far away, so we altered course slightly to port and again increased our speed. The following bursts were well behind and to our right, so we were through with that battery.

By this time we were near the trenches and as we approached—still of course, with the sun behind our backs—I saw an enemy scout machine diving into our trenches and firing at the troops. It was easy to take him in our stride for home and diving steeply I met him nose on as he turned to make another dive. I nearly hit this machine, for we were approaching each other at something like 300 miles per hour. After firing I saw a burst of steam come from the radiator and he took a steep dive towards the River Scarpe. At the time I thought I had set him on fire and he was going to try to come down in the water to extinguish the flames (this fight took place at under 1,000 feet), but I was attributing thoughts to a dead man, for he bit the earth in No Man's Land, sending up a great cloud of dust, since he fell with the velocity of a shell. This was one of the few occasions when I was sufficiently near to the ground to feel sick at the sight of a vertical plunge to earth of what was, but a few seconds previously, a breathing fellow man mounted on wings of silk, but now unrecognisable amidst the twisted mass; death dealt to him while he was dealing death.

And so we flew home, landed and made our report. Four, possibly five, of the enemy had been brought down before breakfast. We ourselves were untouched save for a few small holes in our wings from the anti-aircraft fire and, by virtue of living on the surface, by turning away our faces and refusing to acknowledge death, by casting off that thin veneer of civilisation with the excuse that we were, after all, as it were, hired assassins in the cause of patriotism, we were able to sit down and enjoy a good breakfast. How marvellously can the human mind adapt itself, how easily persuade itself that its course is right, from a nation to the individual; so that all experience, all knowledge, even religious beliefs can be laid on one side until the lust to kill is satisfied, leaving a charred and blackened earth and the sweet sickly smell of blood.

* * * *

"EXTRACT FROM FIRST ARMY INTELLIGENCE, 16TH-30TH APRIL, 1917.

"Hostile aerial activity has been considerable and the enemy has offered much opposition to our offensive patrols, reconnaissance and photographic machines, whilst our artillery machines have been attacked on many occasions. Many fights have taken place in which both sides have lost numerous aeroplanes, but the enemy losses have been considerably more than our own, especially towards the end of the month.

"On the 30th, four of our Triplanes engaged a large number of hostile machines and shot down five of them, including a red scout, which was probably flown by one of Captain von Richtofen's Flight Commanders.

"In general, in spite of the fact that Captain Von Richtofen's crack squadron of fighting machines stationed at Douai, is opposed to us, our scouts have more than held their own and have shown themselves superior to the best German fighters."

This extract recalls vividly to my mind the daily fights we had against the famous Baron von Richtofen's Squadron, commonly called the "Circus," because it was a mobile unit, being employed on any front where it was most needed. As a rule the patrols of this Squadron numbered ten to fifteen machines in a flight which made the odds heavy against our six machine flights, but nevertheless we worried von Richtofen's crowd considerably and took heavy toll of his pilots. Most of this fighting took place at a great height, anything from 15,000 to 19,000 feet up and always well over the enemy lines. It was a standing joke in No. 8 Squadron that the mechanics of Richtofen's Circus must have suffered from rheumatism from lying on their backs on the damp aerodrome at Douai and watching their pilots shot down. In a morning fight against the Circus we always tried to get to eastward so that we had the advantage of the sun; in the afternoon of course we had this advantage, as it was in the west, and our attack was usually a surprise. This was very necessary as the odds were two to one against us, for if one sailed in on a level with the enemy there was little hope of all pilots coming back: better to take a little longer over the job, pick off one or two of the enemy and live to fight again. You will see how very important it was in such fighting for each pilot to select a machine to dive at and withhold his fire until the last possible moment, for to fire at considerable range seldom damages the enemy but gives him excellent warning of the attack. Possibly over an hour has been spent getting into the right position for the attack and this would be entirely wasted by premature firing.

Of course, conditions were not always ideal enough to allow one to obtain the most favourable position, clouds often screened the sun and then one had to use them as cover, but, as the enemy were doing the same thing, surprise was always likely on both sides.

The enemy had their own methods of defence and were the first to use decoy tactics. These were introduced comparatively early in the war with no little measure of success. A favourite method of decoy practice with them was to have a slow two-seater machine flying at a fairly low altitude, say 8,000 feet, while above it at about 12,000 feet would be a formidable array of fighting scouts, and no sooner had an enemy pilot commenced to attack what he thought was "easy meat" when down would come the scouts, with every chance of wiping out the whole English flight. Baron von Richtofen employed a very good plan to catch the unwary Flight Commander; he arranged for four of his machines out of fifteen to detach themselves from the main body as soon as hostile aircraft were sighted. These four machines would appear to fly off as if falling out of the patrol to go home, but in reality they climbed up into the sun, and when the English formation was busy scrapping with the main body of ten to twelve machines down would come the four with every hope of wiping off most of the British patrol. Not a few British pilots lost their lives in this fashion.

For successful fighting it was necessary to know on what work the enemy was engaged and experience gradually taught one to distinguish—for example, there were two-seaters which spotted for enemy artillery, and these would not fly much above 4-6,000 feet; these machines were protected by their own anti-aircraft guns on the ground which, if they saw any hostile aircraft approaching, would put up a warning shot somewhere near the machine. It was, therefore, rather difficult to bring these machines down as, once they were warned of our presence, surprise attack failed and one had many times to be satisfied with driving them away and so preventing them from doing their job.

There were other two-seaters of a very different type, fast machines possessing great climbing powers; their mission generally was photography well behind our lines and long distance reconnaissance and they were very difficult to shoot down on account of the height at which they operated. I have found these machines as high as 19,000 feet, and at this height manœuvre was more difficult than at a lower altitude owing to the more rarified atmosphere; a sudden turn at such a height might, easily make one drop into a dangerous position. In spite of the difficulties, a fight against one of these machines was usually quite a thrilling affair; one was so cut off from the world, nearly three miles above the earth's surface and almost out of sight of the naked eye. A victory over one of these was particularly valuable, as the enemy were robbed not only of two highly skilled men and a valuable machine, but also of the undeveloped photographs of our lines and positions, which might prove of such value that the whole course of war on one front might be affected.

I have made no mention so far of twin-engined aeroplanes and, although on one or two occasions daylight raids were carried out over England in these aeroplanes, as a general rule their scope was limited to night operations. A certain amount of night fighting was carried out against these machines, but there were comparatively few victories owing to the difficulty of finding them in the dark. If an enemy Gotha passed across the moon one could then possibly keep it in view or if one got near enough to see the red hot exhaust pipes glowing one could engage the enemy, but one had to remember that these enemy night fliers were heavily armed, some even having a gun tunnel pointing downwards to guard attack from underneath.

The act of firing one's guns at night made one a perfect target to an enemy, for he had merely to fire at the point whence he saw the tracer bullet coming; it was thus that Flight-Commander Little lost his life at night, while testing his guns preparatory to attacking a Gotha.

Towards the end of the War, scout aeroplanes were used for low flying raids against enemy aerodromes, troops on the march, transport or any form of enemy activity and this work was decidedly unpleasant, for the air was full of all manner of projectiles and one became a target for anyone's fire. On these raids we carried, in addition to about 2,000 rounds of ammunition, four 16-lb. bombs which we dropped on the hangars of the enemy aerodrome or on gun teams, trains, or in fact anything which looked as if it might be improved by the addition of 16-lb. bombs. Personally, I was always relieved when I had found a suitable resting place for this cargo, because I did not relish being hit by a bullet on the bombs and being thereby given a free pass to the next world, providing my own cordite for the job.

What I have told you gives, I fear, a very brief outline of scout work from the Flight-Commander's view in No. 8 Squadron, but I think I have shown you what great need there was for co-operation between Flight-Commander and pilots. One advanced all the time with the science of aerial fighting. Each day brought something new; perhaps it would be a new type of enemy scout, or perhaps a new plot of the enemy to decoy the unwary. Fighting did not cease when a pilot climbed out of his aeroplane on the aerodrome; his mind carried on in thought, developing fresh methods whereby he could defeat the enemy.

I do not wish to conclude this outline without paying tribute to the Squadron Commanders under whom it was my privilege to serve in

No. 8 Squadron. The first Squadron Commander (now Group Captain) G. R. Bromet,
organised the original Squadron. He was
a born leader and one whose leadership inspired efficiency and whose personal example
counted for so much in those days when the
schoolboy was flung into a world where moral
standards were, like everything else, suffering
from the heat thrown out by the cauldron of
war. Next, was Squadron Commander Chris-
topher Draper, a man whom I should
have no hesitation in describing as one of
the finest pilots in the world in his time; to
see him handle an aeroplane was to view a complete mastery of a machine, in which few others
have expressed so much grace of movement. He
gained the loyalty of all, for he was everybody's
friend.

Nor can I conclude without paying my tribute
to all those pilots it was my privilege to lead.
Some led flights in their turn and came through
safely, others were lost in the common cause,
but all were imbued with the team spirit; each
gave of his best and backed his leader up
through thick and thin, so that he could bring
all his energies to bear on the main object, which
was to bring down, drive down, or prevent from
working, all enemy aircraft within the sector one
had orders to patrol.

This spirit and team work, this co-operation
and single mindedness of purpose, under the
able leadership of our Squadron Commanders
earned for No. 8 Naval a name which few

squadrons possess. For, referred to in Sir Douglas Haig's Despatches, congratulated by the Admiralty and the Army Council, it had just cause to be proud of being made a permanent Squadron, when the Royal Naval Air Service and Royal Flying Corps were amalgamated into the Royal Air Force.

CHAPTER IV.

THE FLYING OFFICER

By Captain E. G. Johnstone, D.S.C.

(Flight Sub-Lieutenant R.N. with No. 8 Squadron R.N.A.S.)

CHAPTER IV.

The Flying Officer

"Critics who speak of what they have not felt and do not know have sometimes blamed the air service because, being young, it has not the decorum of age. The Latin poet said that it is decorous to die for one's country; in that decorum the service is perfectly instructed." — SIR WALTER RALEIGH, "The War in the Air." Vol. 1.

It was at Dunkirk that—in R.N.A.S. days—most of the new pilots from England were congregated. We were fresh from an intensive course at Cranwell, and bursting with half digested information, most of which was never the slightest use to us. This was fortunate, because the rapidity with which we crammed for our examinations was more than matched by our power to forget everything just as speedily. Much of our knowledge was important to us, but, for instance, having doggedly mastered the little ways of the Lewis gun, it was a trifle embarrassing to arrive at one's squadron and to discover that the only machine gun used was the Vickers, with which one had only been permitted a bowing acquaintance. It was amazing, however, how eventually everything seemed to turn out satisfactorily.

In 1917, No. 12 Squadron formed the pilot's pool at Petit Synthe Aerodrome, near Dunkirk. R.N.A.S. Squadrons in the field drew on No. 12 to fill their vacancies, and fresh officers from England were sent out to keep No. 12 up to strength. During their period of waiting, the new pilots' only duties were to maintain high patrol over Dunkirk itself, ostensibly to drive off the enemy's high photographic machines, which from time to time came over to observe the results of the numerous night bombing raids or the effects of the shelling by the long range gun. By some dispensation of Providence, there were, to my knowledge, no recorded instances of these enemy aircraft coming into fighting contact with the high patrol. Be this as it may, the work kept the pilots occupied and also gave us this additional flying experience, which we sadly needed.

Eventually, the day came when one was summoned to the Squadron Office and informed of being posted to such-and-such a squadron, and that a car would shortly arrive as transport. To anybody who had set their heart on flying scout machines, it was at this moment a relief to know that No. 8 was a scout squadron, as until then there was always the fear of being sent to fly heavy two-seaters or night bombers.

The car journey down to the new Squadron was a revelation to most of us. To see at first hand all the evidences of war and to realise that within a very few days one would actually be over the enemy lines was to feel that at last training was over and usefulness was about to begin. Upon first arrival at the Squadron's aerodrome, the freshly-joined Sub-Lieutenant reported to the Commanding Officer, and was introduced to the Mess. Everyone did his best to make him feel at home, and the Flight-Commander, no doubt politely disguising his opinion that if appearances were any guide he was not going to be much use, gave instructions to report to-morrow for a preliminary tour of our sector of the lines. Our new pilot retired to his "cabin" (a Nissen hut) with plenty to occupy his mind. To-morrow he is to cross the lines, and to-night a real live Squadron Commander actually bought him a drink. His feelings on this latter point will be more readily understood when it is realised that until that glorious moment no "two-and-a-half striper" has ever betrayed knowledge of his existence, except under official circumstances.

There was one lesson which had to be learned by every pilot who joined the Squadron and the sooner he learned it the more useful he was and the longer he lived. It was essential to realise that, no matter how fine a fellow he thought himself to be, he knew very little about flying, less of active service conditions, and absolutely nothing at all about fighting in the air.

As soon as the Flight-Commander felt that this was understood, he knew that there was some hope. He knew that he could train his new man in his own way and he knew that the man would learn. The flights which proved the most successful were composed of pilots who reflected their Flight-Commander's training and who knew his methods. This does not mean that individuality was destroyed, but that the flight operated as a team under its captain, and that individual brilliance was controlled and diverted into the right lines, and not allowed to become its own undoing.

The first tour of the lines was generally sufficient to bring it home that there was a great deal one did not understand. A preliminary study of the map was of some assistance, but it seemed hopeless to think that one would ever know the way about, and as for fighting, attacking and being attacked, these were possibilities which seemed appalling. Gradually, however, our sector became intelligible as the various landmarks were memorised, and some fine day the new pilot was considered sufficiently safe to be allowed to go on patrol with the flight. Before taking off, the Flight-Commander invariably issued his last warnings—to remain in strict formation and, above all, to keep a sharp and constant look-out.

These two rules seem reasonably easy to obey, but it is difficult to convey to anyone not experienced how extraordinarily hard they are in practice. It is a common occurrence for a new pilot to lose completely a formation of four or more machines, especially after a series of turns or on a cloudy day. He may have had his attention distracted by some peculiarity on the ground, or by what he thinks may be an enemy machine, and meanwhile his leader has dived three thousand feet, followed by the rest of the flight. At such moments let us hope that, if the formation is really nowhere to be seen, our new pilot will turn round and go home. Otherwise he is likely to run into trouble, thus adding to the long list of flying officers who have failed to survive their first fortnight.

The other great difficulty is that of keeping the look-out. With the best will in the world, it is not for some time that it is possible to see half of what may be happening—or about to happen. Many a pilot has landed from a two-hour patrol during the whole of which he has never seen the enemy formation which his Flight Commander has been trying so hard to cut off, or, worse still, has not noticed the five enemy scouts hovering over the two-seater which he was so upset to see allowed to go free. In short, experience is the only guide of value, and I would venture to assert that it is the most exceptional pilot who is anything but a passenger in his flight for at least the first six weeks. One day, however, there arrives an even newer pilot than oneself, and then is tasted that sensation of superiority which, however ill-founded, more than makes up for the period of feeling that the difficulties were almost insuperable and that a state of inexperience seemed permanent.

The above will have given some idea of the feelings of the new pilot. Once the settling-down process is completed it is astonishing how valuable knowledge is picked up day by day. To work behind a capable Flight Commander, who uses his brains not only in the air but also on the ground, and who is not averse to answering questions after the patrol is over, is to receive an education which will in all probability be the direct means of saving one's life, or at least of avoiding risking it, at some future date. No. 8 Squadron was particularly fortunate in its Flight Commanders and as almost all of them previously served with the Squadron as ordinary flying officers I believe that we built up a tradition of flight tactics and of leadership which were transmitted through the different flights by educating the officers along the lines which experience had indicated to be correct. Further, apart altogether from the officers, the same spirit animated the ground staff, with the result that we gained enormous confidence in our fitters, riggers, armourers, and all those who directly or indirectly kept us up in the air. We knew that whatever wanted doing would be done smartly and efficiently and by their keenness our flight hands gave us the impression that we were all one team, each of us playing for the side and doing our very best in our own respective places. On landing from a patrol after taxying to the hangars and switching off the engine, the nearest man would ask, "Any luck, sir?" and close behind him would be the armourer, anxious to know how the guns had worked. To be able to report that we had shot down an Albatross and that the guns had fired to perfection was to see that our mechanics were every bit as pleased as we were. The loss of a pilot was felt as keenly on the Mess Deck as amongst the officers themselves, and a decoration bestowed on any individual was rightly taken not only as a personal honour but as belonging to the whole of the flight and to the Squadron itself. I cannot express too clearly the very real debt which every officer owed to this spirit of unhesitating keenness.

In the previous chapters accounts have been given of the usual patrols which formed our main work. Apart altogether from flight operations, until 1918 it was possible to indulge in a certain amount of private warfare. That is to say that when the day's patrols were completed, one or two of the more experienced pilots were allowed to go off on their own, either to attack some announced objective or, more often, to lay in wait for some particular enemy machine which it might have been noticed formed a habit of crossing our lines or working at the same hour every day. It was curious how persistent was the German trait of working to a time-table, and how we were able consistently to shoot down two-seaters which habitually did the same thing at the same time. One would have imagined that after a while they would have arranged escorts or even laid traps for us, but though naturally we occasionally got the worst of the bargain, generally speaking these individual efforts were extremely successful.

Another important duty with which we were entrusted was the interference with enemy wireless machines. Two pilots were constantly in readiness on the aerodrome, alert at a moment's notice to get into the air. Word would come that an enemy two-seater was spotting for their guns in a certain named area. Our two machines would immediately take off and proceed to the spot as quickly as possible. With any luck they would establish contact with the German wireless machine and, if they were not able to shoot it down, they almost invariably drove it so far behind its own lines that it was entirely unable to carry on with its work of spotting.

We were also used as escorts to our own two-seaters, when engaged on long reconnaissance or bombing raids. Sometimes there would be twelve or fifteen of them, and ten or twelve of us, and the combined formations were distinctly impressive. As long as the engine continued to function satisfactorily, an escort was quite pleasant work, since although one would see plenty of Germans, they would generally keep at a respectful distance and rarely attack such a formidable combination. If, however, one of our machines lagged behind or turned back, the position was not so attractive, and the pilot often had a hard struggle to get home.

In a previous chapter description has been given of a typical offensive patrol. Such patrols formed the bulk of our duties. The following are one or two incidents which may throw light on other aspects of a pilot's work.

The date is November 1917. The weather has been bad for some days, but in spite of this patrols have been carried out practically without interruption, although almost no enemy machines have been even sighted.

The German Air Force at certain periods of the war showed a distinct disinclination to fly or fight more than was absolutely necessary, and if the weather broke they would—so it seemed—gratefully accept the excuse for a few days on the ground.

We made use of this tendency, and on bad days our machines which spotted for the guns consistently flew over the lines, often battling with terrible weather conditions, but generally undisturbed. The gallantry displayed by their devotion will be more readily appreciated when it is understood that these "spotters" were almost invariably a distinctly unstable and dangerous machine, the R.E.8.

These "Harry Tates"—as they were inevitably re-christened — had a pleasing little trick of catching fire if crashed, and I well remember one very windy day when I had been forced to land on a R.E.8 Aerodrome owing to having received a bullet through my petrol tank. Flying conditions were abominable, and I watched four R.E.8s land, all within half an hour. Two pulled up safely, one crashed on landing, and the fourth turned over on the ground. In both latter cases the machines immediately burst into flames, killing pilots and observers. A tribute is due to the squadrons using these machines, and while we scout pilots laughed at them to their faces, behind their backs we heartily respected and admired them.

The Officers' Mess at Mont St. Eloi was composed of two large Nissen huts, joined together in the middle by a square wooden building of nondescript architecture. To adopt theatrical terms, the curtain rises to disclose the officers of the squadron taking their ease after dinner. The gramophone is playing, a game of poker is in violent progress, and the general flow of conversation is punctuated by such remarks as—

"—and went into a spin right away."

"—I don't care—Phyllis Monkman is marvellous in the new show."

"—Four kings! The next round's on me."

"—When's the next Canadian Mail due, Whitey?"—and so on.

It is this cheerful moment of the day, when everyone is care-free, that our Wing Commander selects to send us our orders for the following day's warfare. Like a messenger from the Gods in a Greek play, but rather differently mounted, a motor-cyclist arrives as it were from Heaven and discloses to us poor mortals the particular brand of Hell which we are to expect on the morrow. Generally a notice on the board is sufficient to break the news to us, but on this occasion our Commanding Officer comes in and indicates that he wishes to have a talk to us. He explains that the Infantry are to indulge in a big push towards Cambrai and that half-a-dozen pilots are to set out — individually — to

Sopwith " 1½ Strutter "—110 H P Clerget

Sopwith " Pup "—80 H.P. Le Rhone

Nieuport Scout—80 H.P. Le Rhone

Sopwith Triplane—130 H.P. Clerget

Sopwith " Camel " - 150 H.P. B R. I.

watch the main roads ten miles or so behind the German lines. Our instructions are to report concentrations or heavy movements of enemy troops and to do our best to harass their communications. The pilots to do this work are selected and final orders given. The rest of the squadron will, we are told, carry out offensive patrols as usual, to prevent the Hun doing to us what we hope to do to him.

This sounds as if the next day is likely to be interesting and eventful—to put it mildly—and the squadron, to fit itself for the stern work ahead, goes to bed earlier than usual. At least five minutes earlier.

By all the rules of story-telling, the day of the great offensive should dawn fine and clear. But unfortunately not so—it dawns foul and windy, with clouds at about 500 feet all over the sky. It will be appreciated that if the clouds are at this height, a pilot, to see the ground, cannot fly higher. Five hundred feet is low enough to make a machine a target for every kind of fire from the ground. Archie—the anti-aircraft gun—will have those clouds ranged to an inch, and altogether the prospect of a jagged piece of steel or an ounce or two of lead in some intimate portion of the anatomy seems more than probable. At such reflections it is realised how true are the immortal lines of the poet who pointed out that it is a lovely war.

The pilots chosen for the low reconnaissance are to set out two at a time at intervals of an hour. We will follow the adventures of one of them, whom we will christen "Brown."

117

Brown had not been out in France very long and, although he had been in several scraps and had helped to shoot down enemy machines, he had yet to "get a Hun" single-handed. His taking-off time is 2 p.m., and as this hour draws near he gets into his flying gear, after searching his pockets to see that he has no document on him which might prove of assistance to the enemy if he were captured. With the same idea in his mind, he places his service hat and a pair of shoes in his machine, avoiding in this way the possibility of having to finish the war hatless and in a pair of thigh-length fleece-lined flying boots. He folds conveniently the map of the roads he is to cover, gets into his machine and takes off.

Crossing the trench area he catches glimpses of our infantry. Someone gives him an encouraging wave. He has never before been over the lines as low as this. Landmarks which are distinct at high altitudes are unrecognisable or non-existent at 500 feet. Fortunately, Brown has been warned of this by his Flight Commander and has a compass-bearing in his mind which gives him his direction. These thoughts are rudely interrupted by the sound of a machine gun, apparently directed at him. A couple of slight turns, an alteration in height, and he is past. From now on every minute is marked by machine-gun fire from below. Fortunately, Brown does not happen to go over an anti-aircraft gun battery, or he might be given something to worry him.

He is flying along one of the usual straight French highroads, bordered on either side by the stumps of trees. So far, all seems deserted, but in the distance about a mile away there is something on the road. Brown tests his guns by firing three or four rounds from each, and hopes for good hunting.

What luck! Reserve troops on the march toward the lines. Brown climbs as high as he can without entering the clouds and then puts his nose down towards the head of the column. No one could miss such a target. With a savage feeling of delight, the triggers are pressed and the troops scatter. Mowing them down, Brown flies straight along their once-orderly lines, finishing his burst of fire and pulling out of his dive only a few feet over their heads. A climbing turn, and he is on them again. By this time the road is clear except for the dead and wounded, and the target is nothing like so compact. Remembering that he carries four sixteen-pound bombs he drops these in a line along the hedge in which as many as possible of the Germans are taking cover. This operation being conducted from an average height of fifty feet, he almost succeeds in blowing the tail off his own machine. At least, that's what it feels like. But who cares? All four bombs go off with four satisfactory bangs, and when he turns again he sees that he has been more than fortunate in obtaining direct hits all down the hedge. With a final burst from his guns, Brown sails away, hoping that one German, at least, saw him place his thumb to his nose and spread his fingers out.

It occurs to him that he should go home and report. Something of a reaction has set in.

But a glance at his clock shows—incredibly—that it is barely a quarter of an hour since he left the aerodrome. Besides, he has quite a bit of ammunition left, which it seems a shame to take home. He decides to follow his road a little further.

Five minutes flying towards Berlin fails to disclose any other target worthy of the name. Truth to tell, Brown is now slightly above himself. There are several parties of men, and a gun or two moving up towards the trenches, but in his present mood he is looking for bigger game. For instance, he feels that the Kaiser and Hindenberg ought both to be seizing this opportunity of visiting the Western Front. What a good time he could give them! Unfortunately for his dreams of glory, they fail to oblige. While pondering over this piece of bad luck, he sees another machine, half in the clouds, away to his right. Maybe this is his Flight Commander who took off with him and who is covering another main road not far away.

Brown swerves off right-handed, making for the other machine which is flying in the same direction as himself. Some inner prompting urges him to make a semi-circle and to approach it from behind. This is just as well, since he suddenly recognises it as a Hun two-seater, an L.V.G. He realises, with a thrill, that now is his chance to put into practice the various points he has been given regarding attacking two-seaters. His great difficulty, as he sees in a flash, will be that they are both flying so low that space for manœuvre will be limited.

Just exactly as his Flight Commander told him, he flies down to come up under the enemy's tail, where the Hun observer cannot get his guns to bear. He manages this move to perfection and is just about to press the trigger when the L.V.G. makes a sudden turn and at the same time opens fire on him with its rear gun. An old hand, obviously.

If anyone ever fires at you, the golden rule is to move, and move quickly. Brown pulls up into the clouds, which are only a hundred feet or so above, and then, changing direction slightly, dives again in the hope of getting in a burst from his guns as he takes the enemy by surprise. He succeeds fairly well, but his fire does not seem to do very much harm. Again the Hun evades him, and pours back a stream of tracer bullets which come unpleasantly close. Backwards and forwards, round and round they go, and it begins to dawn on Brown that he can't have very much ammunition left. His blood is up and he determines to take a chance and to settle matters—or be settled.

Ignoring all the rules of aerial combat, and throwing to the winds the precautions which have been drilled into him, he seizes a favourable opportunity and dives straight on the Hun's tail. Withholding his fire until the last possible moment, in spite of all the German observer can do, he puts a burst right into the enemy pilot's cockpit. Fortune is on his side. The L.V.G. rears up into the clouds, and as quickly emerges in a vertical nose-dive. Brown watches, almost hoping against hope that the Hun will pull out and save himself. But a cloud of dust marks the spot where the German hits the ground, his engine full on. The noise of the impact is distinct. Brown, feeling a little shaken, looks over his machine and observes with a curious feeling of nausea that his right bottom plane is torn, and that one of the instruments on his board has been smashed. A close call!

Our friend now thinks that he has done a full day's work and that even the most exacting of Squadron Commanders can hardly blame him for "packing up." The only difficulty remaining is that he has not the faintest idea where home is. His road, which he was following, has completely vanished, and his compass, which should give him at least the direction of our lines, is waltzing gaily round in a most unfortunate manner. Nothing he can see on the ground looks at all familiar, which is hardly surprising considering the fact that he is twenty-five miles over the lines, at a height of two hundred feet. Visions cross his mind of all those pilots he knows, or has heard of, who disappear and are presumed to have landed on the enemy side. It seems long odds that he will add to this number, especially as his engine just then gives a warning splutter and begins to fail.

Quickly! Turn the petrol tap over to the auxiliary supply. That will last for twenty minutes or so. No sooner said than done—and the engine picks up again. Life is at its blackest when the compass shows signs of settling down, and at last gives a more or less steady reading. If it can be trusted, a half-turn to the left should have him flying towards our lines. Over with the rudder—there is no time to be lost with less than twenty minutes' petrol in the tank.

For ten minutes nothing eventful takes place. Several targets are observed on the ground, but for obvious reasons they must be ignored. Brown tries to find some landmarks to fix his position, but everything seems completely strange. Trenches, support lines, begin to show up, and he knows he must be getting nearer home. A minute or two longer, the usual machine-guns from the line, and he is over our own side once more. In front he sees a British machine, apparently making for its aerodrome, and remembering the old adage of any port in a storm, he decides to follow and land to find out his whereabouts. A little later his wheels touch the ground, and as he switches off his engine in front of the hangars he suddenly feels a hundred years old and tired out into the bargain.

Mechanics run up. He gets out, enquires the way to the Commanding Officer's quarters, and goes off to report. The C.O. is interested and, incidentally, informs him that he has landed fifty miles north of his own aerodrome. A telephone call is put through, and in half-an-hour or so he has the pleasure of speaking to his own C.O., reporting his safety and giving particulars of the troops he has shot up and of the Hun he has shot down.

Hoping to get home that night, he walks back on to the aerodrome to find someone to fill up his machine with petrol. There is a small crowd of mechanics round the "Camel," and as he approaches they make way.

"Sorry, sir, but it's not going to be much good filling her up. Look at this—and this."

"These" are not pretty. A fuselage longeron all but shot through, and a main spar almost in halves. The machine will never fly again; in fact it is amazing it flew at all since the scrap. Brown turns away towards the Mess, and it comes as something of an anti-climax when he hears later that when he landed he had only a tea-cupful of petrol left in his tanks.

· · · · · · ·

The above experiences are founded upon fact. Perhaps they will convey some idea of the Squadron's work. No idea can be successfully given of the affectionate mutual regard and esteem which gave the Squadron its spirit and which made us all, officers and men, anxious to do our best, for fear we would fail each other.

CHAPTER V.

THE ARMAMENT OFFICER

By Captain D. W. Pinkney, M.B.E.

(Lieutenant R.N.V.R. with No. 8 Squadron R.N.A.S.)

CHAPTER V.

The Armament Officer

"Arma virumque cano."

I notice in the above quotation that the poet put the arms before the men, though I feel sure that it must have been the exigences of scansion which made him do so. But if the men who use the arms should, and do come first, their weapons are of vital importance too.

In the following few pages I sing the modest song of an Armament Officer and his duties. It all seems to have happened in a former life, but I will try and give an accurate account, so that it may serve as a record of happenings, awake a few memories, and perhaps be useful to present-day armament officers.

After a series of unsuccessful efforts to become a service pilot, observer, tank officer, and other things, I came to the conclusion that an apparent (but by no means real) defect in eyesight must in my case be allied to an obvious lack of intelligence. However, to cut a short story shorter, I heard that the job of Armament Officer to a Naval Squadron on active service had possibilities, and went all out for it.

I was eventually appointed to No. 8 Naval, a fighting squadron whose reputation was second to no other. The job's possibilities immediately became apparent, and were without limit.

During my training at Eastchurch, beyond the usual instruction in machine guns, firing gear, sights, bombs and ammunition, I could find no one able to tell me exactly what I would have to know or do. The real answer was very simple.

The guns were expected to fire so long as the triggers were pressed, and the bombs drop whenever the release gear was pulled. That was the Armament Officer's urgent job.

His subsidiary duties, which included the care of ammunition, aerial and bomb sights, signal lights, revolvers and a staff of armourers, were a matter of routine and training.

His main and pressing job was to get and keep the guns firing.

There was a very good reason why the preliminary training for an Armament Officer to a fighting squadron was inadequate. The fact was that the guns were designed to be fired on land and in a stationary position. Actually they were being used whilst moving at anything up to 300 miles an hour, rising and falling in the air, whilst at the same time the lubricant of gun and gear, also the ammunition, were being subjected to extreme changes of temperature. The guns will jamb on land when in normal use. It was obvious that they would do so in a greater degree in the air.

The Squadron was using pairs of Vickers light machine guns, lying parallel on the fuselage just behind the propeller, the firing mechanism being the Sopwith-Kauper Interrupter Gear. The bullets from each gun had to pass between the blades of the propeller, which would be revolving at say 1400 revolutions a minute. Consequently a propeller blade passed the mouth of each gun barrel about 2800 times per minute.

To fire the guns by means of an interrupter gear was in itself an unnatural way of working them. Furthermore, the speed of the propeller put a tremendous additional strain on the firing mechanism of the gun, because the interrupter gear was taken directly off the propeller shaft.

It is clear, therefore, that the slightest fraction of a "hang fire," the smallest hold-up or slackness in the Sopwith-Kauper gear, or a minute delay in the firing operation caused by frozen lubricant, would certainly result in a holed propeller.

Many cases are known of propellers which had their blades sheared off entirely. In any case a propeller with one or more holes pierced through its blades was in danger of breaking up, or of becoming so unbalanced as to affect its even circular movement, and so cause great vibration and also upset the running of the engine.

If a pilot had reason to suppose that his propeller had been holed, he would have the additional anxiety of knowing that at any moment one or both of his blades might carry away, and either smash up part of the wings or fuselage, or put him at the mercy of enemy aircraft or anti-aircraft gunfire.

This question of holed propellers was almost as important as that of gun failure, and raised many new problems.

Towards the end of my time in the Squadron, a method was found of doubling the rate of fire of the guns. The wear and tear was consequently terrific, and raised a fresh series of troubles which had to be overcome.

Pilots told me that the effect of the first scraps they had with this gun was to chase the Huns right out of the sky for several days. The effect produced by the speeded-up gun was terrific, and the great disadvantage, if any, of this new development was that the ammunition became exhausted in a few moments.

When timing the gear on the ground by turning the propeller over by hand, it was found best to allow the gun to fire when about two to three inches of propeller blade had still to pass the barrel.

With the engine running, the bullets would then clear the blade.

In addition to the above difficulties, conditions in the field were so various, types of machines were being changed and guns, gear and ammunition were being continually modified and altered.

Consequently no set rule could be laid down for an Armament Officer to follow. The job was a new one, and I really think that every one of them more or less made his own.

The fact that the guns were bound to jamb from time to time was no excuse. There was a good and sufficient reason for every failure, waiting to be discovered and put right.

The Vickers light machine gun, which we used, is a marvellous and delicate piece of mechanism, and before setting out to cure its failures when hurriedly adapted to aerial work, it would have been an excellent thing to have had six months' training in the factory. As it was, we had a few weeks' training down at East-church, which embraced many other things besides machine guns, and included the conduct of funeral firing parties. Even those jambed on more than a few occasions.

It is easy now to imagine what a tremendous problem this question of armament supervision must have been to H.Q. Not only had suitable men to be found, but there was only time to give them the shortest of trainings.

It was not even possible to buy any technical books on the subject of machine guns—they had all been bought up.

I remember during my training at Eastchurch feeling more and more ignorant as the time drew nearer for leaving.

Coming up to London one day I met a soldier in the train who appeared to have handled machine guns. I flooded him with questions, but as we had no parts with which to demonstrate, I could not get much out of him. I did, however, extract one or two useful bits of information. His final advice to me was, "You press the trigger, and if it works—it works." "And if it doesn't?" "Well, if it doesn't, it don't—and if you try to go too far with it, it'll bite yer." And if you handle a Vickers lock on a dark night with cold hands, it very often does bite, more efficiently than a bull dog.

But I do not wish to reflect on the training at Eastchurch; it was excellent. Anyone with a mechanical mind and a keenness for the subject could learn as much as an average brain could absorb in the few weeks available. And for one thing I will give them full marks. They did expect us to go into the air and use the guns there. It is, I suppose, possible to learn everything necessary on the ground, though I doubt it. But it is exceedingly difficult to get a pilot to take any advice about his guns if he knows that the giver has never been in the air. It takes some practice for an observer to get used to aerial firing, but the pilot has so many other urgent matters to attend to that he can only give a portion of his mind to the guns. And unless the gunnery officer has been up and tried it himself, he will never properly realise the pilot's point of view and his difficulties. In fact, to be efficient, an armament officer should become a pilot.

One of the most useful sources of information as to gun trouble was from the pilots themselves. And to obtain this, tact and a knowledge of humans was indispensable.

It is highly understandable that a pilot having gone up to 17,000 feet, waited there in intense cold and starved of oxygen, cruised about until fatigued in eye, mind and body, found his Hun, manœuvred successfully for position, got it, dived on his quarry, and then had his guns fail, was not in a fit state to make a technical explanation, or submit to an irritating series of questions on his return.

And what about the pilot who has had a Hun on his tail, been well shot up, and then succeeded in getting into an attacking position, only to find his triggers give no response?

I used to try and be out on the aerodrome whenever machines returned from a flight, and I am surprised now, when I come to review it all, that none of them ever let me have a well aimed burst of fire before landing. I think they might well have done so.

At this point I must pay a tribute to the pilots of No. 8 Naval. On no single occasion when a pilot returned with his guns having failed him, no matter how exhausting or trying his experience had been, did I ever receive one word of complaint. Only those who have a real knowledge of what the conditions were, can begin to imagine the fine restraint and utter sportsmanship required merely to report that the "guns had jambed," and leave it at that.

It was very necessary to be on the spot when a machine returned, because the pilot could give invaluable information, both as to whether the guns had fired or failed to function perfectly. In view of the continual overhauls and adjustments which had to be made, it was just as important to know whether the guns had fired, as to learn if they had not.

Pilots were expected to learn all about the guns, and how to use them, and they made noble efforts to do so. I received some of my most helpful hints and information from them. But it was neither fair nor reasonable to expect too much from them. I suppose to-day there is time for all fighting pilots to learn as much as is necessary about the guns, which are doubtless better adapted and better placed than they were in our time. But they had also had an intensive training, and if the Armament Officer found himself at times short of exact knowledge, it was obvious that the pilots must be even more handicapped in this respect.

My own opinion is that a pilot in those days could hardly be expected to do more than use the sights correctly, fire and re-cock. To expect him to clear jambs in the air, hampered by heavy clothing, thick gloves and other circumstances which demanded his keenest attention, was unreasonable. The guns were in an almost inaccessible position for him, anyway.

But most of the No. 8 pilots took a keen interest in the working of their guns, and gave me every help in their power and many valuable suggestions.

And gun failure might mean more than an unsuccessful action — it might well entail the death of the man who was trying to use it.

But it was not only vital to get the guns firing. There were numerous improvements crying out to be made in the position of the guns and the sights, the accessibility of the cocking handles and triggers, and the strength and tension of their springs. I found pilots immensely grateful for any changes which contributed to their ease in these respects. Every little point which made for their comfort and convenience rendered their job easier and more successful.

Every pilot was entitled to have his guns and sights and triggers just as they best suited him. After all, the gentlemen who undertake the intriguing job of shooting birds give Messrs. Purdey and other gun makers quite a little trouble in getting things as they like them. The pilots were willing to make the best of things as they found them, but delighted with any small improvements.

As often as not a gun which had failed appeared to be in perfect condition when the machine landed. No jamb was left in position, the gear was functioning, and a ground trial produced a splendid burst of fire whenever the triggers were pressed. In that case the only thing to do was to give the gun a minute overhaul at the earliest opportunity, and ascertain as soon as possible from the pilot what was actually happening when the jamb occurred, the position of the machine, the angle and speed of dive, the temperature, whether any trial shots had been fired to warm the gun, and at what altitude.

I do not know whether it would be of any use to-day, but when on leave I acquired a couple of dental mirrors from my dentist, and found that I could easily examine some of the more awkward corners of the gun with them; on one or two occasions they proved exceedingly serviceable.

Some of the jambs which occurred were quite new, and difficult to trace. Let me give one example which caused considerable loss of sleep to P. O. Downs and myself, and one or two armourers as well. We had a series of gun failures whose cause seemed impossible to trace. The guns in question all had a good history according to their logs; they had all been stripped completely on several occasions and all the alterations necessary had been made; the ammunition was good, the temperature not too cold, and the firing gears also apparently perfect. And yet from time to time the pilots — all experienced and with a good knowledge of the guns — reported jambs which completely held up the firing, but cleared themselves by the time the machine had landed. After several days of brain-teasing telephoning other squadrons and hurried visits to the local Army expert, I was reduced to a state of considering the advisability of trying to take a Camel up myself, and so doubtless end an inglorious career.

For the umpteenth time I sat down and made a list of possibilities which might be the cause of the trouble. I took a spare gun and criminally assaulted it. I filed its gear out of shape, altered the spring tension, mixed tracer ammunition with the ordinary, altered the angle of parts of the lock, and ill-used it in other ways which amounted to assault and battery on Messrs. Vickers' good name. Between each experiment I tried the gun, and it fired perfectly. The gun will, in fact, stand an astonishing amount of abuse without packing up.

And then one day when things were reaching breaking point, a pair of the defaulting guns arrived back on the aerodrome, the pilot having missed a sitting Hun. I climbed on to the machine, complete with dental mirror and a high blood-pressure induced by suppressed blasphemy. Nothing apparently wrong, until I shoved the mirror down one of the chutes through which the wonderful new disintegrating aluminium belt links were supposed to escape, and saw two of them fixed in a loving embrace right across the fairway. The mystery was solved. As the machine dived, an air eddy was formed at the exit of the chute, and the links being very light got held up, then finally mixed in a tight mass, and very soon stopped the firing. Usually as the machines returned home the links cleared themselves, and by the time it got back the chute was free again. I got Jordan to prove this for me, and he succeeded in getting back from a trial flight with one chute completely full of jambed links.

I keep two on my desk now, just to remind me never to try and use my brains when in a difficulty.

A slight alteration to the shape and angle of the chute completely cured the trouble, and left everything nice and clear for the "next please."

I came to the conclusion that in certain cases gun failure might be caused by the firing gear being put out of alignment or held up by some alteration in the shape of the machine. The theory might seem a little far fetched, but it did seem possible that when the machine was in the air, particularly if stunting, the strains on rigging would be quite different from those operating when the machine was at rest on the ground, and so tend to throw certain connections out of truth.

Some of the gun failures were so difficult to account for that there seemed no other possible explanation.

I made as many enquiries as I could regarding the amount of gun failures in our Allies' aeroplanes, and those of the Germans and their Allies, and found that they all had immense trouble in this respect; I believe much greater than in the case of English aeroplanes.

I have mentioned failures and jambs rather freely up to this moment, but am not going to admit inefficiency in the Armament Section of No. 8 Naval, either during my time or that of the other armament officers connected with the Squadron. The number of successful aerial combats and strafes on kite balloons and other offensives is sufficient proof to the contrary. It would not be fair to the unflagging and excellent work done by all the armourers if I did not say that I honestly think no other squadron could claim any superiority to ours in the matter of gun failures.

Failures we did have, but there were periods when things seemed to go well, and at those times we received a full mead of recognition from the C.O. and the pilots. When things were not so good, they blamed the ammunition, the lubricant, and anything else they could think of which did not include myself. If I had not known them so well, I might have considered this a piece of cunning on their part, for nothing could have given the Armament a more potent spur than to assume that they were doing their job all right, and that the troubles lay elsewhere. I never expressed my thanks properly because it was impossible to do so.

Incidentally, I visited as many other Naval and R.F.C. squadrons as I could, and it did not take me long to discover that the sun did not always shine uninterruptedly elsewhere.

Without being unkind or untruthful, I can say that I learned very little from the Army on the subject of machine guns and their jambs. I visited as many squadrons as I could, particularly those which I heard at conferences were having a bad time with gun failure. Their pilots told me nothing, like the sportsmen they were, and always vowed that all was well. But the armament officer and myself were very soon shedding tears together.

And yet, whilst the experience was very valuable and I got confirmatory evidence of the cause of some of my own troubles, I learned very little that was new.

And the reason was nothing to do with me. It was simply that the guns which came through to us were in many ways in better condition than the Army ones. Consequently the R.F.C. had a tremendous number of straight-forward jambs, plus the unusual ones, whilst we had for the most part only those peculiar to aerial firing.

One of the most trying things the Armament Section had to face was the fact that the guns kept coming through with all the old necessities for adjustment. In spite of reports, requests, drawings, recommendations and personal visits, none of the minor modifications necessary ever seemed to be incorporated in the next batch which came along. But every now and then some alteration would be incorporated, of which I had had no previous warning. Of course it was inevitable, and easy to understand to-day, but it was great fun at the time.

There was, however, a most refreshing side to the Naval supplies as compared with the Army. When I wanted anything badly, we telephoned Dunkirk, and either it was sent up promptly on a lorry, or we rushed a motor-bicycle down for it. My unfortunate Army contemporaries, however, had to fill in request forms with an immense number of carbon copies, and often repeat the performance with yet more carbon duplicates, and whether they ever got what they wanted I don't know. But, thank Heaven, our supply machine had been decarbonised, fitted with live wires, and was beautifully timed.

I think Warwick Wright, now Col. Warwick Wright, D.S.O., had much to do with this. At any rate, whenever I see his name written in large letters across our railway bridges, I drink to him with my eyes as I pass under them, remembering the urgent telephonic request I made one day to Dunkirk for some new re-coil springs. They arrived within half-an-hour, and Dunkirk was about five hours away by road. You cannot beat that.

Does it spoil the story if I say that the delivery was made to us in mistake for another squadron which had ordered them the day before? I hope not, for Dunkirk was wonderfully quick and well organised.

I have written rather generally about the armament job in the foregoing pages, and will try to particularise a little in the following paragraphs.

I actually joined No. 8 Naval on the 27th September, 1917. Booker and I motored up together from Dunkirk. It was a freezingly cold day, which encouraged him to sit back without a rug and his coat well open at the neck and enjoy himself. The car was an open tourer, and did not loiter by the way. On our arrival he invited me to have a drink; I tried to reply suitably, but the words froze on my lips as it were. Bookie was apparently warmer and more cheery than when we started.

I took over the Armament Section from Pat O'Hagan, an old and efficient hand at the game. He left, after I had extracted as much information from him as I could. His cross-examination was severe if necessarily short, and he certainly was a willing witness. After he left I felt lonely, until P. O. Downs appeared; and he did me a lot of good. He was one of the loyalest and most conscientious petty officers in the service, and the Squadron was lucky to have him. Two hours with a file seemed to do him more good than four hours' sleep; and the rest of the armourers were without exception a real willing crowd, who never failed to do their best, and if ever I was in a tight corner, I could always apply to C.P.O.

Rosling for willing help and the use of his lathe or any other tools required.

The system we followed and tried to develop was as follows :—

A log was kept of every gun, and its behaviour on every flight. Its faults were recorded, and the measures taken to put them right. This was invaluable, and the more correctly the log was kept, the greater the efficiency obtainable.

Every new gun which arrived was taken down, various small but necessary alterations made to it, and a thorough trial on the ground was given.

At the same time the sights were tested and adjusted, and the opportunity taken to test any new lots of ammunition which had arrived.

I always tried to get the guns fired in the air on a test flight, if possible, as there often seemed to be further adjustments necessary which did not become apparent on the ground.

Most careful supervision was given to filling the belts with ammunition, and a record was kept of any faults which were reported on subsequent firing. Separated cases, misfires, and expanded cases seemed to run in batches, and were always reported to the supply base.

After every flight when the guns had been used, they were cleaned, overhauled and oiled, the locks taken off and examined, chutes examined and firing gear cleaned and tested.

A record was kept of every propeller which

was holed, and examined in conjunction with the log of the guns and firing gear which caused it.

A log was also kept of each individual firing gear and its apparent or assumed faults.

Every gun was fitted up with cocking handles, and the position and tension of the triggers and the height of the seat adjusted to the needs of the individual pilot using them.

A journal was kept of any suggestions from pilots, armourers and other squadrons, arising out of the behaviour of the guns, firing gear and ammunition.

Pilots were always asked for a brief report on the behaviour of the guns, and an attempt made to find out the exact state of affairs when any trouble had occurred.

Reports were sent in to Dunkirk at regular intervals, stating what the general performance of the guns and gears had been, and making any necessary comments on the behaviour of the ammunition.

Careful drawings to scale were made of suggested improvements, and full reasons given for recommending them. Owing to the fact that the Squadron included budding engineers, draughtsmen, and representatives of other professions, I was furnished with excellent technical material and drawings; the latter were largely contributed by Peachey.

I think some of the suggestions were found useful. Let me give an example. In one case I evolved an idea for spotting and positioning aircraft in flight at any altitude. This gadget included a racer, round which were set out degrees of the circle from 0 to 90 degrees. I was very proud of this, and when on leave I followed it up to the right department at the Admiralty. The machine was recovered from a cupboard for my inspection, and when the dust had been removed I found that someone had written in succession all round the various degrees the words, "She loves me" and "She loves me not." It had obviously, therefore attracted favourable attention, and I hope that the pointer always stopped at the right answer.

I will not detail any of the technical alterations which were made to the guns, as they are now out of date, and no doubt the present guns have been fully adapted to aerial work.

As regards the ammunition, a series of experiments was conducted to test the effect of differing temperatures. A few hundred rounds were left out during a week of frosty nights. One batch was left a foot above the ground, one on ground level, and one buried a few inches below the ground. Their surrounding temperatures were taken at intervals during the night. Corresponding batches were kept in my dug-out at a temperature of about 60 degrees.

The results were inconclusive, and in spite of exact notes being kept of results obtained when firing, no data of a useful nature was obtained. The ammunition showed very little variation from the normal.

I wonder if the present-day pilots are expected to arm themselves with revolvers on their flights? Ours always did, and it was remarkable how some of them seemed to get lost in the air. After all, it must have been very difficult to find a revolver again, if it had been mislaid at 15,000 feet on a foggy day.

.   .   .   .

At one time I was given quite a lot of interest in our famous concert party, the "Eight Navals." We were a talented and active crowd, and Draper was its life and soul. The following are some of the items which made a frequent appearance on our programmes :—

OPENING CHORUS.
    "Here they come."
SQ.-CD. C. DRAPER.
    "The Tin Gee Gee."
    "If the Wind had only Blown the Other Way."
    "The Naughty Little Bird in Nellie's Hat."
    "Bob down, you're Spotted."
A.M. HAMMOND.
    "How We Saved the Barge."
    "The Lighthouse Keeper's Story."
    "The Caretaker's Story."
FLT.-LT. COOPER.
    "The Policeman's Lot."
A.C. CLARE.
    "Ventriloquism."
O.S. DEMPSEY.
    "Where Did That One Go."
L.M. O'DRISCOLL.
    "Dear Old Home of Mine."
A.M. COZENS.
    "Stewed Prunes and Prisms."
A.M. ADAMS, A.M. BENNING.
    "Melinda's Wedding Day."

A.C. HART.
    At the Piano.
A.M. CLARE, A.M. EWINS.
    Thought Reading and The World's Worst Wizards.
A.M. AVENT.
    "Burlington Bertie."
A.B.A. LEIGH.
    "Cuckoo."
LT. PINKNEY.
    Recitation Competition.

A. M. Uden excelled at painting the scenery, and there were other artists whom I have not remembered as I have mislaid many of the old programmes.

Our performers were occasionally overcome with attacks of modesty, and I had to use my best persuasions at times to induce them to appear. But my final argument, "Do your bit for the good of the Squadron," was always a winner.

My clearest memory of the concert party is that of a bitterly cold night at St. Eloi with a gale threatening to carry the big tent away. The footlights flickered and frequently went out, gusts of icy wind swept through the audience, and froze the performers who were waiting their turn. The tent was crowded with visitors from neighbouring units, and though the wind threatened to put out the lights altogether, it did not drown the constant sound of the guns. Yet no handicaps of stage, lights, lack of rehearsal, or bad weather could prevent that particular concert from being a memorable success.

All our usual artistes excelled themselves. Compston recited "If" in a way that gripped the audience with an obvious emotion; Draper sang his "Tin Gee Gee" and several encores amid tremendous applause. And when it was over we had numerous requests to give a similar show at other units.

My story is ending. But I cannot help mentioning the loyal affection which the splendid leadership of Squadron-Commander C. Draper inspired in all ranks. I joined the Squadron at the moment he took over its command, and as it had been moulded and built up under the influence of Squadron-Commander Bromet; there is nothing to add to that. No squadron could have wished for a finer officer to form and command it. He had the wonderful knack of getting the best work out of everyone, of making all hands feel that every job was well worth while. We all knew he was a glutton for work himself, and he had the rare gift of commanding on service lines men who had not been brought up in the Navy, and showing them what a fine and fair thing proper and reasonable discipline can be.

Draper carried on the good work, and enthused it with his unique personality and power of winning the keen loyalty and great personal affection of us all. I only served a week or so under Squadron-Commander Bromet, and the rest of the time under Squadron-Commander Draper. But there was no break in the continuity of the Squadron's activity. We had exchanged one commanding officer whose out-

An Officers Group taken just after the Armistice

(Below)
Captain R. McDONALD,
R.A.F.

(Above)
Lt. J. H. D'ALBIAC,
D S.O., R.M.A.

(Below)
Flight Sub.-Lt.
R. L. JOHNS, R.N.

(Above)
Flight Sub.-Lt. H. DAY,
D.S.C., R.N.

standing merits we all admired, for another who seemed fully qualified to carry on. We knew Draper already, and were prepared to see him exercise his unparalleled power and knowledge of flying, his keenness and enthusiasm to carry on and add to the Squadron's already fine reputation. We know how splendidly he did so.

It must also be recorded what an inspiration to the Armament Section was the magnificent work done by the pilots of my time. To take a few names at random Compston, Johnstone, Jordan, Munday, Price, Cooper, Booker, Day, McDonald. But they were all wonderful, and they all had a cheery word for the armourers.

I remember good old Canadian McDonald as he climbed into his machine to do a real dirty job of work. He gave me his usual cheery grin and said :—

"Guns all right, Pinkie?"
"Think so."
"I'll just bet they are."

That was typical of "Mac." Always the optimist, always cheery and convinced that everything would be all right. Unfortunately, that flight was his last.

Who could forget Johnstone and Jordan indulging in imitation scraps in the air? The mere remembrance of those hair-raising stunts gives me the old thrill again. Those combats, I might say, were almost invariably continued in the mess. There they took the form of prolonged wrestling matches. They lasted until both parties were completely done, and after each had tried his level best to break the other man short off at the waist. Chairs and tables were overturned in the process, and the fight raged with deadly determination and entire disregard for surrounding persons or things. A stranger would have come to the conclusion that it was the real thing and could only end in murder. We knew better, but they were scraps worth watching. When, and only when, complete exhaustion had been reached, the duel would automatically cease, with honours easy and the friendship stronger than ever. They were both born fighters and leaders.

And then Compston, and his lone quests at heights which he could not really stand. I have seen him so exhausted after such flights that he was hardly able to get out of his machine, and so racked with subsequent headache and depleted vitality that only a long leave could have made up for that continual over-strain.

But he carried on, sustained by an unquenchable fire of devotion, and it is only now these many years after the war that he begins to look less like a physical impossibility. He was a proof that the finest and most successful fighting pilots must be possessed of exceptional brain, sight and spiritual force.

He was the embodiment of the spirit which animated our fighting pilots.

. . . .

Will anyone write a record of the evening binges which relieved the end of a foggy day?

When Johns would shamelessly appear in the guise of a W.A.A.C. going home on leave; when Jordan walked his imaginary quarter-deck, and gradually provoked everyone to struggle in deadly combat with everyone else; when Johnstone—always ready for trouble on land and in the air—had a duel with Jordan, the weapons being Pyrenes; when Cooper played and sang snatches of the latest London shows in his charming way, and suddenly reduced us all to an attentive silence with a painfully pleasant glimpse of life at home; when Draper would take charge of the piano and inspire us all to yelling choruses and happy forgetfulness; when we worked the "funnel trick" on an American General and filled his riding breeches with water, having mistaken his one modest star for the badge of a lieutenant; when Dixon delivered his only and historic speech, and Roach would make sure of his mess bill with a game of poker.

They were wonderful evenings, and like all the best and fullest moments of life, they came unrehearsed and full of sudden and unforgettable incidents.

Johns was, I think, the greatest natural wit I have ever met. His comments on any unusual situation came as quickly as lightning, and were just as bright and penetrating. They were backed by a strong humorous personality, and a power of comic grimaces and mimicry which I have never seen surpassed.

One night he suddenly climbed up the iron pipe of our Canadian stove, which conducted the smoke straight up through the roof. The pipe was exceedingly hot where he embraced it, and he therefore had to scramble madly upwards to attain a cooler situation. When he had ascended about six feet and was clinging on with both arms and legs round the pipe, it gave way just where it entered the roof, and bent slowly in a graceful curve, with smoke pouring out of its open end. Johns was suspended in mid-air hanging on to it. He remained unperturbed, an extraordinarily funny fixed smile on his face. Then in a curious falsetto voice he made an impromptu speech, which started, I remember, as follows :—

"Now lads, when I was aboard the French frigate Flossie. . . ."

And then followed a ludicrous description of life at sea, which reduced everyone, including the long-suffering stewards, to helpless laughter. I would give a good deal to remember it all. He had somehow contrived to take a drink up with him, and his final touch was to appear suddenly to notice the smoke which was still pouring out of the pipe, and then make a pretence of putting out "a fearful fire which was raging in the 'tweendecks" by emptying his glass down it.

His humour gained a great deal by the speed at which his mind worked, and the unexpected twist he would give to the ordinary course of conversation. One morning an engineer came up to Johns, saluted, and reported "Sorry you won't be able to go up, sir; your engine's gone dud." He instantly turned to the C.O., saluted, and with an exact imitation of the engineer's manner, said, "Sorry, I shan't be able to go up, sir, my Camel's got the hump."

One night he appeared as a witch, in an astounding costume, the head-dress consisting of a gramophone record cardboard cover pulled down over his face. It just allowed his eyes, nose and mouth to show through the hole in front, and a large bunch of hair to stick out through the back. He was armed with a pack of cards, and offered to tell anybody's fortune.

Jordan asked for his, and Johns shuffled the cards and laid the three of hearts on the table. He gazed at it and said : "Ah! the Jack of Spades, I see. That means you have had a fatal illness from which you probably never recovered. Let me regard further. (Pulling out the Queen of Diamonds.) Ah! I'm glad we have got the Ace of Hearts; that means you will pull through." And then looking at Jordan's attenuated figure, he said : "And you look like a ruddy 'pull-through' anyway."

On one occasion I was out with Johns and we passed a French farm. Cooper was leaning over a fence and feeding a friendly cow with some greenstuff. He did not notice us, as we were some distance away, but was considerably startled when Johns yelled at him, "Put that cow down."

I treasure a photograph of him, monotonously repeating "Regrettez, nong comprong" to the guard of a French train who had forbidden him to stand on the platform outside the compartment. It says something for Johns' power of humour that the angry official finally had to give in and laugh too.

I was in an unique position in the Squadron, because I was easily the oldest officer there. I was married and had already been some years in business, and I had no executive control over the flying officers : consequently, they felt free to honour me with many of their confidences and difficulties, babes from school that many of them were. I saw a side of their characters which was naturally impossible for anyone else there to do—and it was the pure gold.

I have lately read a string of war books, which appear to deal in little else but blood, mud and filth. They were all there, of course, but I hope some writer will come along and paint a true picture of the other side of it all. All I can say is that in all the terrors and temptations of that life, those boys came through with honour untarnished and steadfast courage undiminished. Everything was there to shake them morally and physically, and it would have been most natural that some of them should have found the conditions stronger than themselves. But they did not do so, and the finest traditions of the race were vindicated and upheld by them all. And I say that, having seen an intimate side of them which only the circumstances could have revealed.

If I could adequately depict the cheerfulness, efficiency, unselfish bravery, and wonderful comradeship of No. 8 Naval there would be nothing else to say on the subject. I had been out to France before, but the atmosphere of that Squadron was something new to me, and as I have not the combined genius of Kipling, R. L. Stevenson and J. M. Barrie, I cannot begin to do it justice. Perhaps Walworth might have done it if he had lived, but unfortunately he did not. His record with the Squadron was splendid but terribly short.

There never was anything like No. 8 Naval, and there can never be anything quite like it again. Let me give it a friendly motto:—

"GUTS and GUNS."

It exists no more as an actual unit, but I hear it's "Soul goes marching on" as "No. 208 Squadron, R.A.F."; all good luck to it.

Cherrio, No. 8 Naval! If guns did occasionally refrain, your officers and men never failed.

CHAPTER VI.

THE LOWER DECK

By F. D. Hammond.

(Petty Officer R.N. with No. 8 Squadron, R.N.A.S.)

CHAPTER VI.

The Lower Deck

"Wahey—Wahey—Wahey! Rise up and shine!"

These were the words which woke me to life on my first morning with No. 8 Naval Squadron in March 1917 as I lay snug in my blankets on the floor of a French hut at Furnes. Slumbering forms were all around me on the floor, while others more fortunate occupied the two-tiered sleeping bunks around the sides, and I saw the huge bulk of the Jaunty (Chief Petty Officer Rosling) striding over the sleeping forms as he thundered his morning reveillé "Wahey! Wahey! Wakeee!!"

To the needs of the somnolent Samway, Headquarters Carpenter, the Jaunty ministered with a stick and Samway was heard growling "Oi, Oi, steady on with that stick, Chief."

Sleep had been intermixed with dreams—and my mind had wandered through the night back over the route by which, I had found my way to No. 8 Naval Squadron. The road had been by way of a few hectic weeks at the Crystal Palace, where in language more lurid than polite I had been taught that the first necessity of the Service was to look after oneself and if necessary then "Pull up the ladder, Jack."

Here it was that the physical instructors, prize fighters all, with an almighty fine specimen for a chief instructor had first put the wind up us. The familiar scene rose before me of the chief instructor perched upon a raised platform armed with a whistle and a voice like a racing coxswain. The whistle blew, the minor prize fighting instructors immediately yelled and cursed as one person, and energised by fright we rushed towards the palings, tearing off coats hats and jerseys as we ran, hung them on the fences and raced back to position in the line tying our braces round our waists at the last moment, hoping to avoid the punishment meted out to the slow-moving mugs who were found absent from their places when the whistle of the chief blew for the pandemonium to cease. The "Jerks" which followed sorely tried many a man's physique and gave many wisdom enough to see the doctor next morning with some plausible excuse for dodging the P.T. parade.

The next stage on my way to No. 8 Naval had been by way of the Mechanical Transport Depôt at Wormwood Scrubs, where certain simple souls showed a most benevolent disposition towards enabling me to make a quick fortune at pontoon, and when in a moment of excessive virtue at an adjoining coffee house I offered to stand treat for supper to two of my would-be benefactors they chivalrously refused to permit it, insisting on being sportsmen and tossing for it. It was the odd man out who paid—and there were two of them, you see, with a system.

We were very soon on a draft for France. It happened on a *Friday* and there were *Thirteen* of us proceeding to Tilbury Docks in a tender driven by a boss-eyed driver. Leading Mechanic Harry O'Driscoll drew our attention to the superstitious circumstances and expressed the view that something was sure to happen—and it did. As we stepped out of the tender at Tilbury we were told to return at once as we were all on draft for France.

And so home one day to my Arabella with my new issue of khaki. Arabella busied herself sewing on the red R.N.A.S. shoulder badge on a blue background and similarly the Albatross— the sign of the air mechanic. Arabella had tears in her eyes and fears in her heart. France was an awful place to her. I would surely catch cold, get in a draught or something. My physical comfort could not be ensured unless I could take an umbrella and a clean handkerchief. And then again, she had heard that the Navy was composed of men whose time was chiefly taken up with swearing when they were not fighting —who went to bed with their trousers on, etc., ate peas off their plate with their knives, never used serviettes, and were addicted to similar barbaric practices. But when she bade me goodbye she stood up like a good brave little English woman. And I promised I would write to her often.

We proceeded from Dover to Dunkirk aboard a monitor escorted by Ships of the Navy.

The transport hut at the St. Pol Depôt was a comfortable place in this bitter winter of February 1917—with its tiers of bunks, its Canadian stove well stoked, its piano and its "rummy" atmosphere. Heavy hours of humping petrol, unloading coal from ships in the harbour, intermixed with noisy evenings of music and song. Bill Adams at the piano and Cozens (better known in concert party days as "Stewed Prunes and Prisms") chortling a song about—

"Just as he was giving Mabel a squeeze,
Somebody would come in for a quarter of cheese,
Oh my it made him feel so funny,
He clean forgot to take the money.

And at the most crucial point of the shop assistant's love-making—

Somebody would shout out shop, shop, shop, shop—
Somebody would shout out shop."

All nights were alike at St. Pol—bombs and still more bombs, and casualties were not infrequent.

From St. Pol, as one of the transport allotted to No. 8 Naval Squadron I proceeded to Furnes, on the way to which place Air Mechanic Ted Evans, driving a new workshop lorry, met a railway bridge which obstinately remained low across the road and accordingly crashed the top of his lorry off.

And so at Furnes on this morning in March I found myself, theoretically and in fact, upon the lower deck with the proud rating of Air Mechanic.

The Squadron, commanded by Squadron-Commander G. R. Bromet, then moved to Auchel, near Lillers, to take up duty under the 1st Brigade 10th Wing, where we remained until moving up to Mont St. Eloi, directly behind the Vimy Ridge.

THE LOWER DECK AT MONT ST. ELOI.

Of all the many places from which the Squadron operated there is not one which lives in the memory of the men so vividly as the camp at Mont St. Eloi, situated as it was on the La Targette Road in the devastated country leading up to Neuville St. Vaast and Souchez, with the Vimy Ridge extending directly before us from the battered Souchez Wood towards Arras, and immediately overshadowing our camp the two old broken towers on the summit of the hill of St. Eloi.

It was here we settled down from 7th May 1917 until February 1918, and as a consequence of our long sojourn in one place conditions of life gradually improved; bell tents, with all their discomfort of cramped space, damp earth for a floor and wet muddy beds (if you were near the opening), soon gave way to the more spacious Nissen huts, wooden floors, wooden bunks one above the other, and the whole warmed in winter by those never-to-be-forgotten Canadian stoves.

The great marquee used as a Mess Deck with its mud by day and its dark discomfort by night gave place to a fine, cosy, commodious French hut. A piano hired from Dunkirk and played upon by one or other of our several musicians, Bill Adams, Toby Hart and Jimmy Newing, gave memorable entertainment when flying hours were over—and ultimately, as a crowning glory, a great concert hut was erected and a deep excavation lined with balloon fabric and filled with water provided an excellent plunge bath for the officers.

Adjoining the aerodrome was erected the ship's bell, which with its snow white Turk's Head clanging rope was a continual object of interest and admiration to the numerous and varied types of soldiery who came to see the Navy fly.

We were very jealous of our Naval distinctiveness, set, as we were, in the midst of the Army. We told our time by the ship's bell, we kept to our port and our starboard watches, we had our Naval grog throughout the whole year direct from Dunkirk, our ratings were naval and we had the naval "make and mends," the half day's rests which men actually and in fact used for repairing and washing clothes and doing any necessary cleansing acts, and we very reluctantly gave up our hammocks when at Serny we became No. 208 Squadron R.A.F.

We believed in the Navy; we believed it to be the Senior Service and we steadfastly insisted on our detached position. The mildest and meekest lorry driver caught by a military police-man driving in the wrong direction on a one-way road (a serious offence for a driver to commit, for he could hold up the war for hours if a convoy were met coming from the opposite direction) would lean over the side of his cab and (for the purpose of this respectable record substituting blessings for curses) would say in dulcet tones : "What's the matter with you, you pretty pet——. What, one-way road—who cares—you old darling. You can't touch us you sanguinary lump of earth—we're the Navy, go to Heaven—and bless you."

Our rating was always a mystery to the Army man. One R.A.F. officer persisted in calling a leading mechanic "Chiefy"—and after a football match when a Canadian team had been regaled with Navy rum there was an instance of a quarter-master or some such rank saying to a leading mechanic as clearly as the rum permitted: "I don't know what rank you are—but you're a d—d good sort. I wish I was in your crush."

Our Squadron prided itself in showing Naval hospitality and all our visiting teams went away with grateful recollections of Eight Naval. One picture I see before me. We had given lavish hospitality to sergeants and men of a visiting Army team. They were loth to leave, some were physically unable, and all were loud in song as we carried their carcases very late at night to the lorry standing in the sunken road below the C.O.'s tent. The noise and shouting was im-mense, when suddenly in the middle of it all we saw, standing on the high bank overlooking the road and silhouetted against the light of the moon, the familiar figure of the C.O. silently surveying the send-off of our football guests. Fortunately, our C.O. was a jolly good sportsman and the incident had no painful sequel.

Life on the lower deck was as a man cared to make it—and the majority made it a very tolerable life.

Our complement of men consisted of just over 100, divided into Headquarters, Flights and Transport Sections.

In writing home to my devoted Arabella, my news on matters of warfare and movement was always reassuring if never very true. This was necessitated by the rigours of censorship. On the matter of the calibre and quality, the manners and morals of my comrades of the lower deck, I was, however, able with perfect truth to set her fears at rest, for there was the distance of the universe between the old pre-war type of lower deck men and those who made up Eight Naval.

In all departments of the lower deck were men of education and refinement in the rôles of mechanics, drivers or blacksmiths. Others were doing the most menial jobs as A.C.2s (Aircraftsmen of the Second Grade). Professional men, school teachers, master builders, legal men, business men, employers of labour of various kinds, men from the Civil Service, the Stock Exchange, from shipping offices and Lloyds, craftsmen of many kinds, and of the best kind —all engineers, motor mechanics, carpenters, and riggers.

Aviatik driven down by Flight Sub-Lt. R A LITTLE—April 24th, 1917

Flight-Lt. R. A. LITTLE, D.S.O., D.S.C., R.N.

A FLIGHT
No 8
SQUADRON

Our Captain of the Heads and Chief of the Incinerator was a master tailor from the city of London, to whom we were indebted for the making of our concert party pierrot costumes; our blacksmith was an auctioneer and estate agent; an antique dealer served as an officers' steward; and an old actor as a driver.

Talents were plentiful. There were men who could respectively paint, sketch, act, sing and do ventriloquial turns. Men with musical talents and men who were athletes. I venture to think our lower deck could not be rivalled for its all-round excellence.

In the world of sport names of sportsmen throng to the memory: Squadron-Commander Bromet, our quarter-miler; Jack Black, Peachey, and Brownridge our 100 yards and 220 yards men; Jock Davidson our wonder for the mile; and our dogged Cockney driver Lynn—a sticker on long cross-country work.

In soccer football we had a team which always rendered a good account of itself:—

> GOALIES.—Doc Leigh (the Sick Berth Attendant) and Brownridge (Transport).
>
> BACKS.—Frank Randall (a Chippy), Petty Officer Green.
>
> HALF-BACKS.—Squad.-Commander, Draper, the giant Myddleton (Armourer), the Old Hambone (Transport).
>
> FORWARDS.—Squad.-Commander Bromet (Centre), Jock Ritchie, Taylor, Clifford Crewe, P.O. Bebbington, Rooke and and Needham.

We played as many as five football matches in three days. We tackled all types of Army teams and were only once badly outplayed, and that was at Mont St. Eloi by the Canadian Black Watch—a team of hefty Canadian-Scottish giants. We played football at all times of the year even on a hot July afternoon, and we played it among shell holes and on fields of thick stubble.

Cricket was also indulged in, and among the lower deck ratings Bowry of the Transport was the acknowledged stylist. One match was played on some rough ground in the Canadian Camp along the road to Neuville St. Vaast with shrapnel and high-explosive shells bursting around the observation balloons close at hand. The cricketers, in white flannels on a shattered landscape, amid such surroundings made a strange and unforgettable picture. It was only during the Mont St. Eloi days, however, that we had a real series of cricket matches, though subsequently at Tramecourt I remember trying to arrange a match on the aerodrome between officers and the lower deck. The officer to whom I suggested the match was a certain Lieut. F. S. G. Calthorpe, our Armoury Officer at that time. We walked out on to the 'drome—which was a field of stubble. I pointed out the only spot I thought possible and Lieut. Calthorpe ejaculated "My God!" turned on his heels and made for cover. It was not until afterwards that I learned he was the Hon. F. S. G. Calthorpe, the well known county cricketer—and I did not then wonder at his horror at being asked to play on such a wicket.

For our athletes old Ted Evans of the Transport (an old time boxer and sport) acted as trainer—rigged himself up an old hut and gave up his evenings to the massaging and rubbing-down of the runners who were practising for Army sports events. But it was a real sad day for Ted Evans when the C.O. took to horse riding. There was nowhere on the Camp to house the bally horse except the training hut—and so the horse got the hut. Ted Evans had scrounged for miles to get the material—spent all his spare evenings in building it—and lo, he had done it for the C.O.'s horse. Assailed by Evans I had to make an effort. With trepidation I approached the C.O., but the result was the horse had got to stay—there was nowhere else for it. Ted Evans was mad; the runners were up in arms—and I was unwise enough to make a second attempt. I bearded the C.O. in his office one evening. I said, "About your horse, sir." He wheeled on me very sharply saying, "What about my horse." I made a miserable effort, failed, beat a hasty retreat from the office and the C.O.'s horse won again.

THE CONCERT PARTY.

Our Squadron Concert Party was good fun and provided entertainment not only for our own Squadron but also at Casualty Clearing Stations and neighbouring Camps.

Squadron-Commander Draper was the life and soul of the Concert Party and the joy of the Officers' Mess. He brought into all his work such a light-hearted carefree temperament that he radiated merriment. We shall not easily forget the part he played nor lose the remembrance of his happy singing, the favourite song with all being his "Tin Gee Gee" (nothing to do with the C.O.'s horse) and "If the wind had only blown the other way, I might have been a different girl to-day."

Then there was Adams and Benning in song and dance; Cozens (the Sam Mayo artist) who also earned fame by his presentation of "Stewed Prunes and Prisms"; and the good Irishman Harry O'Driscoll, whose fine baritone voice was heard at its best in the singing of those plaintive melodies of his native land which became familiar to us all.

> "She sang the wild songs of her dear native land,
> And lovers around her were sighing;
> Ah, little they dream who delight in her song,
> How the heart of the singer is breaking."

That was the tenor of one of his songs, and Harry O'Driscoll, loyal Irishman that he was, sang it as though his own heart was breaking—and won success accordingly.

Of our officers, we do not forget the versatility of Lieutenant Pinkney, and his crowning success as Mlle. Sans Gêne in light and gauzy finery tripping fairy-like about the stage in classical and other uncensored dances.

And again the clear-voiced Flight-Lieutenant Cooper ("Gladys") singing "The Policeman's Lot is not a Happy One."

OUR RELIGIOUS SERVICES.

Man is of dual composition—he has his gay and his serious sides. The Concert Party catered for the gay side and the Chaplains catered for the serious side.

We would not admit being religious. We always tried to play the game, to shield a pal, to face our gruel when our turn came to take it, and fine qualities of comradeship and a manly sportsmanship predominated in the ranks, but we did not admit that there was any religion in that. By attending a religious service we got away from the camp and duties for an afternoon. Though we often started with this purely irreligious and selfish motive, we sometimes found the atmosphere of the Service a mellowing, softening all-for-our-good atmosphere. Home and wife were seen as it were through the windows of the old hut or marquee in which the Service was being held, and we beheld familiar streets and heard in fancy the church bells ringing, and wondered whether our good Arabella was going to Chapel with the son whom we loved.

In the restful atmosphere of that quiet Service we caught again the spirit of the home from which we had been so long estranged—the love of the wife, and the purifying nature of our child's company.

Some Services I attended were marked by curious incidents. There was that Service in the Casualty Clearing Station at Lozinghem, near Auchel, where the Altar was set against a background of canteen, the mugs and bottles being only dimly draped by the overhanging Union Jack—and where during the Service an absent-minded R.A.M.C. Orderly burst into the hut with pale ale designs and a loud, "Jim, give us a bottle of—" The rest of the sentence died in his lips as he saw his mistake, and crashing the door quickly behind him we heard his boots clattering heavily and guiltily on the stones as he ran away; whilst inside the canteen the pious congregation endeavoured to look as though they had never heard the disturbing voice, nor guessed its beery intent.

And once at Mont St. Eloi when Jimmy Newin and the Jaunty formed the chief actors in a pretty little farce. The Chaplain was at his place, the Jaunty had herded the Flock into the pen which was the Mess Deck, but had forgotten the pianist, our friend Jimmy Newing the motor cyclist. Jimmy had been "blowing" to his pals all the morning as to what he was going to say if the Jaunty asked him to play for a Non-conformist Parson. (Jimmy was Church of England himself and he was going to refuse on the ground of conscientious objections.) Now the Jaunty was not a person whom one would describe as a pious man, but he intended to get this Service going—and the Jaunty knew how to get things done, no man more so. He sent for Jimmy. Jimmy came up from the transport tent with an "I'll see him blowed first" expression on his face. The Jaunty guessed what was in the wind, and before Jimmy Newing could get half a word out, the Jaunty, standing right outside the place of worship, bullied and bellowed in his very finest style, cursing Jimmy for keeping the Service waiting and shouting in a voice of thunder "In yer go! In yer go!" The Jaunty opened the door of the old French hut where the worshippers and the Parson waited, and literally blew poor Jimmy in, slammed the door, smiled broadly at me as I stood watching the farce, and in his great rolling way rolled complacently to the door of his own hut conscious of a duty performed, rolled right on to his bunk, and slept soundly through the Service.

WORKING DAYS.

Though Jack's the boy for work, Jack's also the boy for play. On the lower deck we could work as hard as we could play. That we played hard the bruises of the rugger and soccer football was sufficient evidence. Freddy Power broke the bridge of his nose at rugger and another had his teeth knocked down his throat —mere incidents in the game.

Judging by the casualties on the lower deck we seemed to be exposed to more risks in our play than in our work. We took up baseball, bought a baseball set and tried to emulate the murderous pitching and smashing of the Canadian and Coon players—and I hear once again the sound of that thud when the hard ball, flying from a mighty smash, hit one of the spectators (not a player this time) on the forehead.

The worst real casualty I remember was when at Serny the travelling kitchen — a top-heavy vehicle over-weighted one side with a cooking-range—fell over while being moved, pinning "Bernard" Shaw beneath it. Or again when an unfortunate mechanic, endeavouring to swing a sticky propeller, held it a second too long as the back-fire occurred and, being pulled off his balance, suffered a broken thigh from the backward revolution of the "prop." Sam Wyllie also was a casualty—crashing on a motor-bike between Maretz and Donstiennes.

Both transport drivers and mechanics had some exciting times when salving the engines of planes which had been forced to descend in the shell-swept zones near the "line," but our lucky stars were always in the ascendant. Let it be said to the eternal credit and honour of our pilots—they were the men who faced danger continually and their losses bear silent testimony to that fact. On the lower deck we always took our hats off to our intrepid pilots. Our mechanics, however, gave them the sweetest, safest running engines they knew how, and our riggers did their part in seeing that a pilot went up with the strongest and tautest of planes to carry him through.

Work was eternal, and when there were dawn patrols, men were up a great part of the night working on machines, and in the grey cold hours before dawn the planes were wheeled out ready for flight.

A transport man stood by the ambulance tender, with engine running, ready should a plane crash to race across the aerodrome, pick up the pilot and get him away to hospital without delay.

All day long mechanics were chasing the "birds" over the aerodrome—and in the hot days of summer innumerable miles were run by these men in heavy boots but with clothes reduced to as little as possible below their blue or khaki dungarees. They were tired men when they turned into their bunks at night.

There were no trade union hours for them, and they had to be ready to turn out night or day when duty called. They were busy days when, for instance, ratings were conveyed early every morning from Tramecourt to Izel-le-Hameau to the aerodrome there, and working hard all day were brought back each night to camp. Iron rations every day plus what could be scrounged on our return. In those days our pilots were operating from Izel-le-Hameau aerodrome doing low flying, trench enfilading, and other risky jobs to harass the enemy in the successful attack then being carried out in the country to the right of Arras. It was a heartening sight to see the German prisoners coming in, but the First Aid Stations told the price that was being paid for successes.

After the day's work we retired to our quarters, usually the old Nissen huts. Usually also, surrounded by mud. Two tiers of bunks down each side and down the middle; at the end a window of canvas and the beloved Canadian stove; the lane down each side of the centre bunks a cramped and crowded hive of industry. Twenty odd men, twenty odd kit bags, twenty odd "Primus" stoves, twenty odd petrol tins with one side cut out to form a washing basin, a stewing pan, a footbath or some other vessel of necessity—all in the narrow lane, and all the men active on some job or another. Some washing, some having a footbath, some shaving, some boiling their water preparatory to making a hot cup of coffee, some toasting cheese à la Welsh Rabbit, some cooking savoury onions, bacon, bits of meat, pork and greens, scrounged from old Brearley, the Ship's Steward. Bowry (the man who sent a lorry up in flames) eternally pumping up his "Primus" stove, to the mortal horror of his immediate neighbour who kept his boots on ready to make for the door when the bally thing burst. Men just in from the mud, and bringing mud up the floor; stepping carefully over the evening suppers and hot baths, and being threatened with some dismal discomfort if they mismanaged their feet—and in the corner the little Joe Fagan crying above the hubbub: "Anybody else not had his tot of rum."

The old hut had a smell like mother's scullery on a washing day, a bone-boiling factory, a fried fish shop, a coffee shop kitchen, and a cat's meat shop on a July day, all mixed in one.

The cleaning, cooking, eating and washing-up over, letter writing, leg pulling and chaffing filled up the evening until bed time, and ultimately with the electric lights going out at "Lights Out" quiet was gradually obtained, broken only by some incorrigible gabbler who could not be stopped even by the well-aimed boot or boot brush, and who only subsided temporarily when the door opened and the Duty Officer, accompanied by the Duty Petty Officer, appeared doing "the rounds," at which precise moment silence in the hut was broken only by the snorers.

And so to sleep, dreaming sometimes of the gargantuan feats we should have to relate when we returned to Blighty.

The War was won upon the well-filled stomachs of the personnel. You would not have seen the figure of our Jaunty in those days and doubted this principle.

ERRATA.

        for Flight Sub-Lieut. D. W. Price, D.S.C.

        read Flight-Commander D. W. Price, D.S.C.

APPENDIX I.

CASUALTIES TO PERSONNEL.

KILLED IN ACTION.

Rank and Name.			*Date.*
Flight Sub.-Lieut. W. H. Hope	...	...	23-11-16
Flight Sub.-Lieut. Hon. A. C. Corbett	...		4-12-16
Flight Lieut. A. S. Todd	...	...	...	5-1-17
Flight Lieut. C. R. Mackenzie	...	...	24-1-17
Flight Sub.-Lieut. W. E. Traynor ...		...	2-2-17
Flight Sub.-Lieut. E. B. J. Walter ...		...	24-4-17
Flight Sub.-Lieut. A. E. Cuzner	...	...	29-4-17
Flight Sub.-Lieut. E. D. Roach	...	...	1-5-17
Flight Sub.-Lieut. H. A. Pailthorpe		...	23-5-17
Flight Sub.-Lieut. H. L. Smith	...	...	24-5-17
Flight Sub.-Lieut. F. Bray ...	...	...	15-7-17
Flight Sub.-Lieut. E. A. Bennetts ...		...	7-8-17
Flight Sub.-Lieut. P. A. Johnston ...		...	7-8-17
Flight Sub.-Lieut. A. J. Dixon	...	...	4-1-18
Flight Sub.-Lieut. H. Day, D.S.C. ...		...	5-2-18
Flight Sub.-Lieut. D. W. Price, D.S.C.		...	18-2-18
Flight Sub.-Lieut. C. R. Walworth ...		...	18-2-18
Lieut. W. H. Sneath	...	...	...	6-4-18
Captain R. McDonald ...	...	...	...	8-5-18
Lieut. P. M. Dennett ...	...	...	...	2-6-18
Lieut. W. S. K. Scudmore ...	...	...	18-7-18
Lieut. J. Mollison	...	...	...	27-8-18
2nd/Lieut. C. H. Living	...	...	...	2-9-18
2nd/Lieut. A. H. Hiscox	...	...	...	6-9-18

PRISONERS OF WAR.

Rank and Name.			Date.
Flight Sub.-Lieut. J. C. Croft	...	...	5-1-17
Flight Lieut. W. S. Magrath	...	...	9-11-17
Lieut. D. C. Hopewell	...	...	7-4-18
Lieut. W. E. Cowan ...	...	...	16-5-18
2nd/Lieut. H. K. Scrivener ...	...	...	8-7-18
Lieut. W. E. Carveth ...	...	...	25-7-18
32065 Sgt. D. Totman	...	...	28-7-18
Captain L. C. Gilmour	...	...	31-7-18
Lieut. J. P. Lloyde ...	...	...	10-9-18
2nd/Lieut. J. M. Dandy	...	...	24-9-18

KILLED ACCIDENTALLY.

Rank and Name.			Date.
Flight Sub.-Lieut. S. V. Trapp	...	...	10-12-16
Flight Sub.-Lieut. J. W. McAllister	...	23-6-17
Flight Sub.-Lieut. G. S. Smith	...	...	23-11-17
Lieut. R. L. Johns	...	...	...	11-6-18
2nd/Lieut. S. Clark ...	...	...	17-9-18

WOUNDED IN ACTION.

Rank and Name.			Date.
Flight Sub.-Lieut. E. R. Grange	...	...	7-1-17
Flight Sub.-Lieut. D. Shields	...	...	1-5-17
Flight Sub.-Lieut. L. E. B. Wimbush	...	9-5-17
Flight Sub.-Lieut. E. D. Crundall ...	...	10-5-17
Flight Sub.-Lieut. F. V. Hall	...	...	23-5-17
Flight Sub.-Lieut. W. L. Jordan	...	...	24-9-17
Flight Commander R. J. O. Compston, D.S.C.		4-10-17
Flight Sub.-Lieut. W. M. Davidson	...	27-10-17
2nd/Lieut. G. J. Glazier	...	...	...	15-4-18
2nd/Lieut. J. W. Marshall ...	...	...	2-9-18
Captain A. Storey	...	...	...	26-9-18
Major C. Draper, D.S.C.	...	...	...	13-10-18

INJURED ACCIDENTALLY.

Rank and Name.			Date.
Flight Sub.-Lieut. Preston ...	...	...	23-3-17
Flight Sub.-Lieut. S. W. McCrudden	...	5-9-17
Lieut. M. C. Howell ...	...	...	...	15-5-18
2nd/Lieut. G. Lovett ... '	...	...	...	7-9-18

APPENDIX. II.

HONOURS AND AWARDS.

Feb. 16, 1917.	F/Lt. S. Q. Goble, D.S.C. .... D.S.O.
	F/Lt. E. R. Grange .... D.S.C.
	F.S.L. R. A. Little .... D.S.C.
	F.S.L. M. B. Galbraith, D.S.C. ... Bar to D.S.C.
Apl. 27, 1917.	Sq.-Cdr. G. R. Bromet .... D.S.O.
	Flt.-Cdr. B. L. Huskisson .... D.S.C.
	F/Lt. R. J. O. Compston .... D.S.C.
	C.P.O. H. H. Scott .... D.S.M.
	C.P.O. J. A. Rosling .... D.S.M.
	P.O. H. Dawson .... "Mentioned."
May 11, 1917.	F/Lt. R. A. Little .... Bar to D.S.C.
	F/Lt. R. A. Little .... Croix de Guerre.
May 29, 1917.	Sq.-Cdr. G. R. Bromet, D.S.O., Legion d'Honour.
June 15, 1917.	A.F/Cdr. C. D. Booker .... D.S.C.
	F/Lt. G. G. Simpson .... D.S.C.
July 16, 1917.	Flt.-Cdr. R. J. O. Compston, D.S.C.,
	Bar to D.S.C.
	F/Lt. R. A. Little, D.S.C. .... D.S.O.
July 26, 1917.	F/Lt. R. R. Soar .... D.S.C.
Aug. 18, 1917.	A.F/Cdr. R. A. Little .... Bar to D.S.O.
Aug. 12, 1917.	Flt.-Cdr. C. D. Booker,
	Groix de Guerre and Palm.
Sept. 21, 1917.	F/Lt. R. R. Thornley .... D.S:C.
Dec. 12, 1917.	F.S.L. W. L. Jordan .... D.S.C.
Jan. 1, 1918.	Flt.-Cdr. G. W. Price .... D.S.C.
	F.S.L. W. L. Jordan, D.S.C. ...... Bar to D.S.C.
	F.S.L. H. Day .... D.S.C.
	F.S.L. E. G. Johnstone .... D.S.C.
Jan. 8, 1918.	Flt.-Cdr. R. B. Munday,
	Belgian Croix de Guerre.
	Flt.-Cdr. R. J. O. Compston, 2nd Bar to D.S.C.
	Flt.-Cdr. G. W. Price, D.S.C. ... Bar to D.S.C.
Feb. 26, 1918.	Flt.-Cdr. R. B. Munday\ .... D.S.C.
Apl. 30, 1918.	Sq.-Cdr. C. Draper .... D.S.C.
	C.P.O. W. A. Hill .... D.S.M.
	P.O. H. Dawson .... "Mentioned."
May 20, 1918.	Major C. Draper, D.S.C. .... "Mentioned."
June 3, 1918.	Major R. J. O. Compston, D.S.C. .... D.F.C.
Sept. 21, 1918.	Capt. W. L. Jordan, D.S.C. .... D.F.C.
Dec. 3, 1918.	Capt. J. B. White .... D.F.C.
	Capt. W. E. G. Mann .... D.F.C.
	Capt. A. Storey .... D.F.C.

APPENDIX III.

AERODROMES OCCUPIED

St. Pol, Dunkirk	...	France	... 25-10-16
Vert Galand	...	,,	... 26-10-16
St. Pol, Dunkirk	...	,,	... 1-2-17
Furnes	...	Belgium	... 14-2-17
Auchel (Lozinghem)	...	France	... 27-3-17
Mont St. Eloi	...	,,	... 16-5-17
Middle Aerodrome	...	,,	... 1-3-18
Walmer, Dover	...	England	... 3-3-18
Teteghem	...	France	... 30-3-18
La Gorgue	...	,,	... 2-4-18
Serny	...	,,	... 9-4-18
Tramecourt	...	,,	... 30-7-18
Foucaucourt	...	,,	... 23-9-18
Estrées-en-Chaussée	...	,,	... 9-10-18
Maretz	...	,,	... 26-10-18
Strée	...	Belgium	... 3-12-18
Heumar	...	Germany	... May 1919
Eil	...	,,	... 7-8-19
Netheravon	...	England	... Sept. 1919

APPENDIX IV.

AEROPLANES AND ENGINES.

On formation the Squadron was equipped with—

1 Flight Sopwith two-seater ("1½ Strutter")—110 h.p. Clerget engine.

1 Flight Sopwith Scout ("Pup")—80 h.p. Le Rhone engine.

1 Flight Nieuport Scout — 80 h.p. Le Rhone engine.

On 16-11-16 the Squadron received 6 Sopwith Scouts ("Pups"), 80 h.p. Le Rhone engines, to replace the Sopwith two-seaters ("1½ Strutters").

On 20-12-16 the Nieuports were replaced by Sopwith Scouts ("Pups").

On 1-2-17 the Squadron handed over all its aeroplanes (18 Sopwith Scouts ("Pups")) to No. 3 Squadron, R.N.A.S.

At the end of February 1917 the Squadron commenced to re-equip with Sopwith Triplanes, 130 h.p. Clerget engines, and went down to the R.F. Corps on 28-3-17 equipped with 16 of these machines.

At the beginning of July 1917 the Squadron commenced to re-equip with Sopwith Camels, 130 h.p. Clerget engines, and by 12-7-17 had two flights of Camels. By 6-9-17 the re-equipment with Camels was complete.

During February 1918 the Squadron re-equipped with Sopwith Camels, 150 h.p. B.R.1 engines.

The Squadron was re-equipped with Sopwith Camels, 140 h.p. Clerget engines, on 11-4-18.

On 8-11-18 the Squadron commenced to re-equip with Sopwith Snipes, 200 h.p. B.R.2 engines, and was completely equipped by the end of November 1918.

APPENDIX V.

COMPOSITION OF No. 8 NAVAL SQUADRON.
October 26th, 1916.

HEADQUARTERS.

Squadron-Commander (Acting) G. R. Bromet,
In Command.

Flight-Commander B. L. Huskisson ... 2nd in Command.

Lieutenant J. H. D'Albiac, R.M.A. ... Records Officer.

2nd-Lieutenant V. P. Spurway, R.F.C.,
Equipment Officer.

W.O. II. T. G. Brice .... Stores Officer.

Sub-Lieutenant H. O'Hagan, R.N.V.R.,
Armament Officer.

Flight Sub-Lieutenant N. R. Cook,
Spare Pilot and Ground Officer.

"A" FLIGHT.
Six 80 h.p. Le Rhone "Nieuports" 17.B.

Flight Lieutenant C. R. Mackenzie.

Flight Sub-Lieutenant R. J. O. Compston.

,,	,,	H. L. Wood.
,,	,,	G. G. Simpson.
,,	,,	Hon. A. C. Corbett.
,,	,,	A. H. Lawson.

"B" FLIGHT.
Six 80 h.p. Le Rhone Sopwith "Pups."

Flight Lieutenant S. J. Goble.

Flight Sub-Lieutenant E. R. Grange.

,,	,,	W. H. Hope.
,,	,,	D. M. B. Galbraith.
,,	,,	S. V. H. Trapp.
,,	,,	R. A. Little.

"C" FLIGHT.

Six 110 h.p. Clerget Sopwith "1½ Strutters."

Flight Lieutenant J. C. P. Wood.
,,   ,,   C. E. Hervey.
Flight Sub-Lieutenant G. Thom.
,,   ,,   C. D. Booker.
,,   ,,   H. Jenner-Parson.
,,   ,,   R. R. Soar.

120 C.P.O.s, P.O.s, and Men.

APPENDIX VI.

Copy of signal sent by Wing-Captain C. L. Lambe to No. 8 Naval Squadron on its formation on 25th October, 1916 :—

I much regret that I am unable to personally wish good luck to officers and men of the Detached Squadron. I wish to point out that the Squadron has been selected to operate on the Somme Battlefield under conditions requiring skill, hard work, and endurance, and I feel confident that officers and men will put up with any discomfort without complaint, and will uphold the honour of the R.N.A. Service. I wish the officers and men the best of luck and hope to visit them in the course of a week or so.

APPENDIX VII.

APPRECIATION OF NAVAL SQUADRONS ATTACHED TO THE R.F.C.

The following message was received from the Secretary of the Admiralty through the Commodore, Dunkirk :—

"Sir,—

"I am commanded by my Lords Commissioners of the Admiralty to inform you that they have received, through the War Office, the following expression of appreciation from Field-Marshal Sir Douglas Haig of the services rendered by Squadrons of the Royal Naval Air Service at present with the Expeditionary Force :—

" 'The Pilots have shown energy, gallantry and initiative, and have proved themselves capable of standing hard work and hard fighting. Further the machines with which they have been provided have undoubtedly helped largely towards the success of the aerial fighting which has taken place this spring on the front of the British Armies in France.'

"The Army Council endorse this appreciation and add an expression of their own thanks.

"2. I am to desire that this may be made known, through the appropriate channels, to the Officers and Men concerned.

I am, Sir,

Your obedient Servant,

(Sgd.) W. F. NICHOLSON,
for Secretary."

APPENDICES VIII, IX AND X.

These consist of remarks on the future design of Scout machines and notes on aerial fighting by Flight-Lieutenant C. R. Mackenzie, who was killed early in 1917.

It is considered that these are of particular value and well worthy of inclusion in the history of the Squadron. Written as they were at the end of 1916 his remarks on design show great foresight, and his views on offensive formation flying should prove of the greatest interest, both as a record of the best practice at that date and as still containing advice which remains sound even to-day.

APPENDIX VIII.

Remarks on Future Design of Scouts and Suitable Armament for them.

By FLIGHT-LIEUT. C. R. MACKENZIE.

Though it is foolish to speculate into the far future, it is necessary to anticipate the developments of the immediate future. The Scout alone concerns us.

1. In aerial scout fighting to-day the greatest asset a machine can have is speed at a height. This is absolutely of essential importance, both in attack and defence, and constitutes far and away the most important asset a scout can possess.

2. The next most important asset to a scout is its offensive armament, to enable you to make sure of the enemy machine once your speed has put you in position. You should not need defensive armament if your speed is sufficient; of course sometimes you will meet a scout faster than yourself and you will probably go under unless the rest of the formation can help you. To-day a scout mounts one gun only, and that a modified gun, not specially designed for lightness. The cartridges are the same as those used on land, i.e., with effective range of 600 yards and actual range of three miles. All that is required in the air is a cartridge with fairly effective range of 200 yards. One looks forward to the day when the invention of a specially light gun, with specially light cartridges, designed to be effective over a range of 200 yards only, will enable three guns and 150 rounds per gun (all that is necessary) to be mounted in a scout with the same weight as the single Vickers gun and 400-475 rounds of ammunition. The trouble of synchronization would be overcome by placing a gun inside the two layers of fabric in the planes just to clear the propeller. The barrel would presumably have to traverse the main spar, and the weakening thus caused would be an objection to the scheme, but perhaps not an insuperable difficulty. A disintegrating belt would be inside the plane and some sort of flap would have to

195

be invented to gain access to the gun. The head resistance which is so noticeable a feature of the modern gun would be reduced to a small hole in the leading edge. With regard to the jambing of guns. If a gun were driven off the engine, all jambs, except "vital ones" such as double-feed, would be obliterated; jambs caused by the spring, defective charge and the cold would not occur. The gear should contain one weak spot which would break at a certain strain, then if a vital jamb occurred, the gear would not be much affected. It is suggested using a rimless cartridge to get over jambs caused by separated case. These cartridges would be cast in one piece as in the .450 revolver cartridge.

It would not seem impossible to produce a scout machine carrying eight guns to be fired singly or from one trigger, calibrated to fire parallel, thus immensely increasing the field of fire and leaving any machine attacked by a scout in an extremely precarious position. If it were found that the mounting of several guns in a scout impaired its performance so much as to render its speed too small to escape when attacked, suitable two-seaters could be mixed with the formation for defensive purposes.

3. Every scout machine of the future must have a good climb in order to reach the altitudes where combats occur. An exceptional climb is, however, a very useful extra quality to possess. Thus the Sopwith Scout's best method of breaking off an engagement is to climb, as she has not got a sufficient superiority in speed to escape some German machines, while her climb is remarkably superior.

4. Visibility is a great asset both in attack and in defence, and also in keeping station.

5. Handiness is always very useful but given speed it is not essential, it is of importance to be able to make easily the slight movements necessary for sighting.

6. Strength is essential, if a pilot is to have full condence in himself and his machine as a fighting unit.

7. It is a very great help to be able to lose height quickly, but not essential.

8. Enough attention has never been paid by designers to standardising, i.e., throttles should be approximately in the same position in all makes of machines, and should open in the same direction. All machines should have a map case built in.

9. The trigger must in all cases be on the joy stick and the cocking handle accessible.

In conclusion we can look forward to the ideal scout of the future as a multiple-gun machine of fast speed at height and a good climb, possessing as many of the important qualities enumerated above as possible. Should the question of mounting multiple guns in practice make the machine carry too much weight (the weight of the pilot carrying out original official tests is never quoted, and this may vary 60 lbs.), it may be pointed out that the fuel capacity could be cut down to $1\frac{1}{2}$ hours and patrols ordered accordingly with advantage. No offensive patrol should mean a flight of more than $1\frac{1}{2}$ hours. Long patrols at great heights with great aerial activity lead to premature loss of nerve and casualties, and have no advantage in them. Finally this type of machine is essentially an offensive scout and should be used for offensive patrols only. It would be folly, for instance, to turn it into an escorting machine or to make it carry wireless. If a designer while designing, building and testing a machine had the constant advice of a thoroughly experienced war pilot, a much more efficient and satisfactory machine could be turned out. This would also avoid endless work in the flights, under the difficult conditions of active service, and would avoid such simple mistakes as not putting the trigger on the joy stick. The experience of this pilot must not be more than a month old. This would also give a good opportunity of resting a pilot after a strenuous time.

APPENDIX IX.

Notes on the Characteristics Desirable in a Scout Pilot.

By FLIGHT-LIEUT. C. R. MACKENZIE.

Every pilot of forty hours flying experience is imbued with the idea that he is a scout pilot. This is highly inaccurate because the scout pilot, who is to bring down enemy machines and at the same time preserve himself and his machine for the use of his country, must possess very special qualities.

1. He must, colloquially speaking, be fearless.

2. He need not necessarily be an extremely accurate pilot with regard to landings, etc., but at an early period of his flying career he must show an aptitude for throwing his machine about, and by the time he has entered upon his active service career he must have done all the commoner "stunts," i.e., steep stalls, loops, side loops, vertical turns, etc.; in fact he must have his machine perfectly under control in any position, and the position of his machine must never be a source of fear to him. These evolutions must be practiced in a suitable machine and never under 4,000 feet.

3. He must be gifted with a perfect head and be able to grasp a situation with special rapidity.

4. He must be, physically speaking, absolutely fit and his eyesight must be perfect.

APPENDIX X.

Notes on Aerial Fighting in Formation.

By FLIGHT-LIEUT. C. R. MACKENZIE.

TYPE OF MACHINE CONSIDERED :
80 H.P. LE RHONE SOPWITH SCOUT.
NUMBER OF MACHINES :—
FIVE.

(a) THE FLIGHT LEADER.

In the first place he must choose suitable pilots to fly together, and having chosen them must let them always fly together and in the same positions in the formation as far as possible. He must endeavour never to let a pilot fly any machine but his own over the lines.

He is responsible for his flight leaving the ground punctually and, to make certain of this, must ensure that all pilots are dressed and comfortably settled in their machines five minutes before the flight is due to start.

All engines having been previously run by the Petty Officer must be seen to be ticking over. Then, on a signal from the P.O. that all engines are satisfactory, the flight leaves the ground in thirty seconds, the order of getting off corresponding to each machine's position in the formation, thus :—

$$1$$
$$2 \quad 3$$
$$4 \qquad 5$$

The leader must fly full out to about 700 feet, and in an absolutely straight direction. He then throttles right down and flies his machine as slowly as possible; meantime watching his pilots pick up the formation (this should not take more than one or two minutes). This done he gives the "attention" signal by rocking his machine laterally, or by firing a red Verey's light, turns and heads to the lines or as he thinks fit and opens up his engine, when the turn is absolutely completed. The formation then begins to climb and the leader must adjust his engine to the worst climbing machine as quickly as possible and having done that, alter his throttle speed and direction as little as possible. He must look round at his formation at least every minute. Do not use a ◇ formation as this leaves three rear machines open to attack instead of two.

(b) THE FLYING OFFICER.

It is of paramount importance for a flying officer to be able to use his throttle to the full and to be thoroughly able to alter the angle of climb of his machine. This sounds extraordinarily easy, but it is the root of the trouble of all bad formation pilots. They will not use their throttle and alter the speed of their machine.

Having left the ground, each pilot picks up his allotted station in order, i.e., as close as possible and slightly above his next in order, i.e., as close as possible and slightly above his next ahead and throttles right down. In flying in a ∧ formation pilots should fly as close as possible together, and the angle subtended by the formation must not be to acute, otherwise the leader cannot see his machines, if they get too far behind him without turning his head excessively, i.e.—

correct	incorrect
∕＼	∧

There is no excuse for a pilot being astern of station and if he is above his next ahead, he must put his nose down and catch up. Having once picked up formation, it leads to endless trouble if a flying officer loses position and starts doing circles on his own. The slightest mistakes in position must be instantly corrected; do not wait until the error is a big one. An exact parallel is found in steering a boat or a car. A good helmsman keeps on his course by employing none but the smallest motions of the tiller. The evolutions of altering course is more difficult. The flight leaders should always endeavour to turn to the same direction, assume this to be left, thus giving each pilot a chance to learn his own particular job.

202

The flight leader rocks his machine repeatedly and pauses and then he does a minute turn to the left, at the same time throttling down and putting his nose down a little. The two pilots on his left do a slight right hand turn throttling down a little more. The two pilots on his right commence a left hand turn, keeping their engines full out. Then the pilots on his left both do a steep left hand turn, the leader turns to the left and the two right hand pilots carry on with their left hand turn. Then the leader straightens out and the formation picks up its dressing and the leader opens his engine and carries on as before. This is far the most successful method of turning a formation.

No further point should present great difficulty on this side of the lines. Pilots must remember to fire their guns as continuously as possible to prevent freezing, keeping in mind the bullet's ultimate destination. Also remember to look behind and towards your formation, thus helping to prevent a surprise attach on the other "arms" of the formation.

On Crossing the Lines.

In enemy territory hostile aircraft and anti-aircraft fire make an accurate formation a matter of some difficulty, and in practice machines fly more in a group than in a formation but the more accurate the formation the easier is the task for the already overworked leader. The leader has to keep his formation together; to decide when to attack H.A. (Hostile Aircraft); to watch for H.A. about to attack; to see his formation does not lose its way; and to attend to many other small points. The flying officer's main duty is to keep formation on the leader and watch out for being attacked; this latter applies most to the two rear pilots.

Signals Between Machines.

These are in practice mostly given by the leader: (a) rocking the machine laterally to call attention to anything; if accompanied by waving the arm it calls attention to H.A. in that direction. If followed by rocking the machine in a fore and aft direction it means a gun jamb. (*b*) A green light means an escort to the lines for engine failure or any other reason.

Never wave except to indicate H.A.

If a pilot wishes to communicate with the leader he must get in front of him and give the signal. If unable to do this he must communicate somehow with another pilot and he will warn the leader. The leader must on no account allow a returning pilot to cross the lines unescorted.

Do not continually call the leader's attention to H.A., he has already seen them probably, and has good reason for not attacking. If a machine gets out of touch with the formation he must go to a previously arranged spot for reforming.

ATTACKING H.A.

The following ten commandments in aerial fighting are considered of vital importance. They may appear cowardly, but they are compiled from the experience of the pilots of this Squadron and many experienced R.F.C. pilots. The man who gets most Huns in his lifetime is the man who observes these commandments and fights with his head. The others either get killed or get nerves in a very short time, and the country does not get the full benefit of having trained them.

1. Do not lose formation.

2. Do not press an attack on a two-seater who fires at you before you are in perfect position. Break away and attack him or another H.A. later with a chance of surprise.

3. Do not stay to manœuvre with a two-seater.

4. Do not dive to break off combat. German machines are better divers but worse climbers than our machines as a rule.

204

5. Do not unnecessarily attack a superior formation; you will get a better chance if you wait five minutes.

6. Do not attack without looking for the machine above you; he will most certainly come on your tail unawares while you are attacking if you are not watching him. Look behind continually on a dive.

7. Do not come down too low on the other side or you will have all the Huns in Christendom on to you.

8. Do not go to sleep in the air for one instant of your patrol. Watch your tail.

9. Do not deliver a surprise attack at over 90 knots unless you wish to scare H.A. off friendly machine's tail. Most machines are not easily controlled at that speed and the firing period passes too rapidly.

10. Do not deliver a surprise attack at over 100 yards range at the very most.

Of course these rules only apply to an offensive patrol. If the hostile machines must be moved, they must be moved at all costs.

Delivering an Attack.

In delivering an attack remember that your most important asset is surprise. The commonest ways to effect this are :—

1. To wait till the enemy machine is going away from the sun and come in on his tail; (2) To dive from a big height; (3) If you have a marked ascendency in climb to come in from below and behind (this method has its obvious drawbacks); (4) To attack while he is obviously otherwise engaged. Thus it is often not wise to attack immediately sometimes. It pays, too, to find out what is the object of the enemy's flight and attack

him whilst carrying out this object, and least likely to be on the lookout, e.g., photography. While he is attacking or waiting to attack a machine, an enemy presents little or no defensive. When shadowing H.A. keep as far away as possible and keep to sunwards of him. Do not forget that a single enemy machine at low altitude is probably a bait and a counter-attack must be expected and anticipated.

With regard to the method of attack it is usually best and easiest to attack from behind. These right angle attacks through the wing are not usually successful. Attacking from in front is not to be recommended. In practice the method of attacking from behind is the one most used. But it is very easy to make a mess of an easy chance. Try and discover if you have the speed of the H.A. flying level (always assuming you are above him) if you have not—glide straight down to him and attack on the steep glide withholding fire until very close, i.e., 100 yards. If you *have*, dive well behind him and come up to him very slightly lower on the throttle. If the attack is a surprise, place yourself about 25 yards behind him, very slightly below, and throttle down to his exact speed, then fire. You want to have one hand on the throttle the whole time and of course the trigger should always be on the joy-stick. This method of attack seems very simple but, as in all things, the more practice the better. It is very easy to lose speed too far astern and be so long in catching up that you are observed, or to have too much speed and shoot by the enemy machine. The most difficult part of all is to withhold fire till the correct moment. Pilots learn their own methods of attack from experience, but this will be found a good one to try, especially in a Sopwith 80 Le Rhone Scout. If, before you are in a position to fire, you see the observer produce his gun, make off at once. Do not stay to scrap and manœuvre with a two-seater. A Scout is designed for offensive and has absolutely no defensive, except its performance. When the leader attacks it is usual for 2 and 3 to accompany him down. 2 is supposed to attack the same machine as the leader, but in practice things arrange themselves. If two machines attack an enemy simultaneously, it more than doubles the chance of success. 4 and 5 remain aloft for a short period to guard the tails of 1, 2, and 3, and then join in, if 1, 2, and 3 are not attacked. It will be readily understood that in the case of one formation attacking another, no rules of combat can be laid down.

A very pleasant help in time of trouble is to put yourself in the enemy's place and view the situation from his point of view; if you feel frightened before an attack, just think how frightened he must be.

ON BEING ATTACKED.

The German will not often attack unless at a very great advantage. If you see a hostile machine above you, try and climb above him; if this fails try and get into his blind spot below the lower plane and then turn and try and lose him. You can always shake him off by going back to the lines, or joining a friendly formation. If you are already in a formation he will probably not attack. If you see that he has got to attack, steer a straight course for the lines, unless that course is away from the sun, and wait for him to dive. Do not turn and twist the moment he starts to dive or he will stop and you will have to go through it again. Wait until he is nearly within decisive range, then put your nose down slightly and do a turn; that is quite sufficient to make him miss and he will probably carry on his dive. If you suddenly hear a machine fire on your tail, do a side loop at once. In all fighting in the air, keep your head, put yourself in the enemy's position, and don't unnecessarily tackle any chance less than an even one.

www.ingramcontent.com/pod-product-compliance
Lightning Source LLC
Chambersburg PA
CBHW030933150426

42812CB00064B/2840/J